Sleeping at
the Starlite Motel

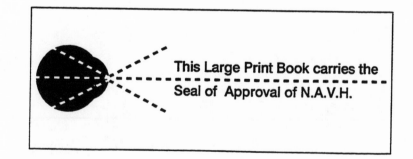

This Large Print Book carries the
Seal of Approval of N.A.V.H.

Sleeping at the Starlite Motel

and
Other Adventures
on the Way Back Home

Bailey White

Thorndike Press • Thorndike, Maine

Published in 1996 by arrangement with Addison-Wesley Publishing Co.

Many of the designations used by manufacturers and sellers to distinguish their products are claimed as trademarks. Where those designations appear in this book and Addison-Wesley was aware of a trademark claim, the designations have been printed in initial capital letters (e.g., Absorbine Jr.).

Thorndike Large Print ® Americana Series.

The tree indicium is a trademark of Thorndike Press.

The text of this Large Print edition is unabridged.
Other aspects of the book may vary from the original edition.

Set in 16 pt. News Plantin.

Printed in the United States on permanent paper.

Library of Congress Cataloging in Publication Data

White, Bailey.
    Sleeping at the Starlite Motel, and other adventures on the way back home / Bailey White.
        p.   cm.
    ISBN 0-7862-0555-5 (lg. print : hc)
    I. Title.
[PN6162.W467   1996]
814'.54—dc20   95-37987

For Rodie

Acknowledgments

I would like to thank Polly Blackford, Roberta Bierry, Rebecca Bridgers, Jeanne Greenleaf, Lucien Harris, Mary Harris, Pacey Hawkins, Katharine Heath, Daryle Jennette, Becky Johnston, Spencer Jarnagin, Eleanor Lilly, James S. Mason, Heywood Mason, Sheila Massey, Rhoda McGraw, June Bailey McDaniel, Henry S. Pepin, Guy Ross, Mr. Russell, the spelunkers, Annie Strunk, Carl Tomlinson, Grace Turpin, Barbara White, and Robb White.

Contents

NATIVE AIRS

SCENIC OVERLOOKS

CLOSE TO HOME

NATIVE AIRS

Civilized Friends

One of my dearest childhood friends has lived for the past twenty-five years in Paris, where she teaches English to French people. I see Alma only once a year, when she comes home to visit her family for a couple of weeks. She calls me up when she gets here, and I go over to her mother's house in the afternoon, and we sit in the living room and drink tea.

Sometimes I try to talk Alma into doing some of the things I enjoy — swimming in the deep springs and sinkholes in north Florida, or just taking a long walk in the woods in the late afternoon. But Alma says that something about living in Paris for so many years has caused her to develop an irrational fear of the natural world.

"But it's not like we're in the wilds of Borneo," I tell her. "What exactly are you afraid of?" I'm thinking if I can comfort her with a few reassuring facts, she will lose her fears.

Alma says, "I'm afraid an insect will bite me, or I'll fall over or be scratched by a tree."

"Well, Alma," I say, "have another cup of tea."

On other visits, Alma tries to talk me into coming to see her in Paris. She describes her fascinating cosmopolitan friends, and peculiar little museums she knows about, and wonderful cheeses.

But I tell Alma I just can't get up my nerve to go there.

"What exactly are you afraid of?" she asks me.

And I say, "I'm afraid I will find myself abandoned in the middle of a busy intersection, and I will stand there and stand there, trying to find the courage to cross the street, and cars will whizz by in five or six directions, and their drivers will blow their horns and shout at me in a language I do not speak. And eventually I will wither up and be blown away like a piece of ash and lost in the gray shadows of a great city far from home."

Alma thinks for a while. "Have another cup of tea, Bailey," she says.

And in the end I don't really regret that

Alma and I can't share the things we love best. I'm just happy that we are so civilized we can sustain a friend twenty-five years on nothing more than of tea and conversation.

The first memory I have in this life is of a blackened and petrified dog, curled up in a glass case in a museum in Pompeii. I remember his humped-up back, his little rat tail, and his amazingly well preserved feet, with the pads and toenails still intact. I do not recall my mother's explanation of the museum exhibits at Pompeii, but it must have been effective, because just as clearly as I remember the physiognomy of that charred dog, I remember comprehending for the first time, gazing through the beveled glass, the meaning of distance and the steady passage of time.

Now the things I see when I am far from home sometimes appear as if they are in a display case, like that dog in Pompeii, and once again I feel the charm of distance. At the checkout stand in a sparsely supplied grocery store near Chinle, Arizona, a filthy dirty man in front of me tells me that since he moved to Arizona from Oregon he has developed painful cracks in the tips of his fingers. "It's the dry," he says and holds a finger. Sure enough there is a deep ed crack. But what I notice is that three of the other fingers are missing completely. Just little stumps are left.

I swallow and say, "Try calendula cream."

In my own town I know the story of every missing body part: an ear in an auto accident, a middle finger in a miscalculation at a table saw, a thumb in a freak accident involving a white horse and a Chrysler coupe. It is one of the joys of distance to realize that I will never know what happened to the three fingers of that man in Chinle, Arizona. As I watch him walk out of the grocery store and into the sweltering parking lot, a bag of groceries under each arm, I can almost see the sheen on the beveled glass front of that dark mahogany case in Pompeii.

In a park in Cambridge, Massachusetts, one summer afternoon I befriend a little old retired Latin teacher. She tells me about the Peloponnesian War and feeds pigeons.

"People don't think much of pigeons," she says, "but they are remarkable birds."

"Yes," I say, "they do have those lovely colored feathers on their necks."

"Not only that, my dear," she says. "They have lovely minds."

But I have to catch a train, so I can't stay to learn more about the minds of pigeons, or the Peloponnesian War, or the Latin teacher's nineteen-year-old deaf white cat with diabetes.

And some winter day, not too long from now, when I'm at home in the Georgia sunshine planting anemones, that old Latin teacher will die in her apartment in Cambridge. In the next weeks, when my anemones are putting up their first ferny leaves, her apartment will be sold, her deaf white cat euthanized, and at 12:15 every afternoon the pigeons will gather in the park and stomp around in the cold on their chubby pink feet. One early spring day, for no reason at all, I'll look at a bunch of anemones on my kitchen table and see that mahogany glass case. There will be the old woman, tossing a handful of seeds and saying, "Not only that, my dear — they have lovely minds."

When I was a little girl I found an irregularity in the wood grain on the end of a bookcase in my house that made a picture of a squealing pig trussed up by his hind legs and dangling head down from a tree limb. When I came home from that trip to Pompeii, I remember scrambling down from my mother's arms and running from room to room in our house, breathing the fragrance of home and looking for that picture in the wood grain. Sure enough, after all that time and distance, the pig was still there. It was comforting, that pig and the smell of home.

And it is still a comfort to come back from traveling, with my random memories like a display in some Victorian museum of miscellany, to a home full of people whose lives I know so well that I can tell the story of every missing finger and call every old lady's cat by name. I've found it's a pleasing balance, the charred dog against the squealing pig.

Family Values

My aunt Eleanor was taking a shower the other day when the whole bathroom fell right through the floor and landed in the dust under the house. Dripping wet and all lathered up, picking soap and tile grout out of her ears, Aunt Eleanor crawled out of the debris and through the startled doodlebugs.

Actually, every good family has a story of a spectacular plumbing disaster. The finer the family, the more wonderful the story.

"Your great-uncle Melville," said Aunt Eleanor wistfully, "came through the ceiling from a second-floor bathroom, right over the dining-room table when Pamela was having her garden club luncheon." She reflected bitterly. "And we have sunk to this."

I knew what she meant. A simple plunge from the ground floor, and no guests in the house at the time. There's no denying that our family has degenerated over the years:

17

the family fortune frittered away, the big house sold. We are probably not up to a second-floor plumbing disaster involving chandeliers and crown moldings.

"Are you all right?" I asked Aunt Eleanor, trying to change the subject. "Do you feel as if all your back bones are fused together from the impact?"

"I feel fine," she snapped, "just humiliated."

"Actually," I said, "nowadays people are judged more by the clothes they wear, the kinds of cars they drive, and where they go on vacation. Determining social status by plumbing calamities has become obsolete."

Aunt Eleanor sighed. "I'm old-fashioned, I guess," she said.

The plumber told her that most houses these days are built on concrete slabs, so there's no potential for accidents like the one she had. He recommended a fiberglass tub and shower unit. "You'll never have another problem," he said.

I went to town and bought Aunt Eleanor a $60 linen skirt and a gold watch. She smoothed down the pleats of the skirt and strapped the watch on her arm. She thanked me, but she didn't look impressed.

"Concrete slab," she muttered. "Fiberglass." She sank into the moth-eaten down cushion on her Chippendale chair, closed her eyes, and let her mind drift back over the years to a time when our family would have been ranked number one in the Grady County equivalent of *Burke's Peerage*, when the women were ladies and wore white lawn, and the men were gentlemen and smoked fine cigars. "Shot right through the ceiling medallion he did, your great-uncle Melville," Aunt Eleanor said dreamily, "and landed in the tomato aspic. Now there's style. There's class. There's breeding."

Ashes

It was a moonlit summer night. From behind the two tea olive trees came a scuttling sound, a little scrape, and a rattle. It was my grandmother, trying again to sprinkle Aunt Rose's ashes in the garden. Then from the upstairs porch my grandfather's voice roared down.

"Ida!"

"Yes, Jaz?"

"I'll not have this sprinkling of ashes!"

"Yes, Jaz."

My grandfather was peculiar about death. He didn't like to acknowledge it, as if he felt that, like the tree falling in the forest, unobserved it would not exist. His resistance made things difficult for my grandmother, who had made a deathbed promise to sprinkle Rose's ashes in the old garden Rose and her sister, my grandfather's mother, had planted in their youth. Unlike her nephew, Aunt

20

Rose had found a kind of inspiration in mortality.

"Your uncle Lund died under that quilt, my dear," she would say cozily, carefully smoothing out the creases. On the mantelpiece she displayed photographs of dead people, propped up in their coffins, looking glum. And on the wall were framed floral scenes in shades of brown and tan, woven from the hair of departed loved ones.

Of course, Aunt Rose had elaborate plans for her own death and dispersal. When she was in her forties she embroidered herself a fine white-on-white linen shroud. And as she lay at last on her deathbed, beatifically wasting away, her old fingers stroking the white silk flowers on the heavy linen, she made my grandmother promise that her ashes would be sprinkled on a moonlit summer night in the old garden of her childhood home and that her favorite poem would be recited:

" 'God wot!' " she murmured frailly, sinking into a theatrical delirium, " 'fringed pool, rose plot, ferned grot . . . Nay, but I have a sign . . . ,' " and she raised a trembling finger. " ' 'Tis very sure God walks in mine.' " Then she closed her eyes and died perfectly.

But for ten years my grandfather's proscription held fast, and Aunt Rose's ashes moldered in their gilt and alabaster urn on the mantelshelf in a downstairs front room.

"I'll not have this sprinkling of ashes," he would command at the breakfast table the morning after every one of my grandmother's attempts. And she would silently bow her head over her oatmeal and calculate the date of the next full moon, when she would try again to keep her promise.

When it got to be my grandfather's turn to die, things were different. Where Aunt Rose had lain in her bed, peaceful and relaxed with a little smile on her pale lips, enjoying the melodrama and the opportunity her own death gave for displays of fine crewelwork, my grandfather lay as tight as a knot, gripping the sheets.

"He's hard to die," people said and shook their heads.

"Don't let him put his hands on me. Don't let him put his hands on me," my grandfather raved. He meant the undertaker, and after he finally died, his wide-open eyes staring at the light, my grandmother had to follow his body to the crematorium, making sure at every stage that the undertaker did not lay a hand on it.

Carrying out the deathbed wishes of lunatics made my grandmother a little impatient with the subject herself, and in the spirit of efficiency she disposed of both Aunt Rose and my grandfather on the same moonlit summer night. She sprinkled Aunt Rose with her favorite little poem, hastily recited, in the old garden, as requested, and nearby, using a posthole digger, she buried my grandfather's ashes in a cardboard box, without ceremony, as he would have wished.

On the subject of her own death she was unequivocal. "Do whatever you want to," she told us. "I just don't want to be *trouble* to anybody," she added with an exasperated sigh. When the time came, it seemed the right thing to do to sprinkle her in the garden with everybody else. No poetry was read, since no one could think offhand of anything fitting, and it didn't seem appropriate to go to the trouble of looking into *The Oxford Book of English Verse*. We sprinkled her ashes in daylight, when no one would have to lose any sleep over it, and that was that.

Years went by, times changed, and the family fortune dwindled. My uncle, who was the last member of the family to own that house, worked for a living and raised four children in his spare time. It was not possible to maintain the formal garden in its 1890s elegance, and weeds spread over the raked gravel paths, the boxwood hedges grew leggy and shapeless, and the fringed pool filled with leaves and muck. Then in the 1970s my uncle sold the house, and it was turned into an inn. Once again people of leisure stroll through the round rose bed, linger under the two old tea olive trees, and sit on the stone bench among the ferns.

It is said that ghosts come out and wander around when they are dissatisfied. Sometimes I wonder about those three laid to rest in the old garden. My grandparents are content and peaceful, I'm sure — my grandfather in the knowledge that none of the strangers walking in the garden knows that he did such a shameful thing as die, my grandmother in the knowledge that maintaining the house and garden are no longer any *trouble* to her family and that my uncle now lives in a comfortable modern house in town. The only one who might come out on moonlit nights and glide around, unsettled, is Rose, wanting some attention. Yet I'm sure every now and then a guest in the downstairs front room must notice the faint rust ring on the mantelshelf and trace around it with her finger and idly think that someone must have set a glass down there one evening and left it overnight, marring the finish.

The Chairs

"It looks like a fungus," said Lilly, gazing up at our cousin Mandon's new house, "some ghastly thing that might spring up out of the ground after a heavy rain."

We stood there shivering and studied the house with its corbeled chimneys and Palladian windows. The house was definitely Colonial in style, but some parts seemed too big and other parts seemed too small, as if it had been designed by someone who had made a careful study of the Tryon Palace under the handicap of a visual learning disability. The sky was gray, the earth was gray, in the distance the Rappahannock River was gray, and the house, in Williamsburg pink brick, did look raw and unnatural sitting there on the scarred ground with old snow piled up like dirty rags around its base.

"He wants our chairs," Eleanor said darkly.

We were here in Virginia, Lilly and me

and our old aunt Eleanor, together with five more distant cousins, because of eight Chippendale chairs. There had been twelve of the chairs originally, made in 1750 for an ancestor of ours in Jamestown. Over the years four had been lost, and the rest had drifted around in the family and ended up in the possession of various scattered cousins. Mandon, our richest cousin, had made millions of dollars in the cable TV business and within a year had had this house erected on an old estate in Virginia's northern neck, complete with dependencies and a straggling avenue of newly planted Bradford pear trees. Now he had tracked us all down and organized this gathering of the chairs and their owners.

"New money," said Eleanor, eyeing the ill-proportioned downstairs windows with their snap-in muntins. "That man thinks money can buy anything."

Eleanor had no money herself, but she had the remnants of wealth — a few pieces of fine old furniture, a couple of threadbare Herez rugs, a complete set of chipped up Meissen china, and her nineteenth-century notions of etiquette and good taste, about as useful in 1993 as the grammar rules of a dead language.

"He'd love to get his hands on your chair,

Lilly," Eleanor said. Lilly's was an end chair, with arms and a richly carved splat.

"Do you think so?" asked Lilly. "I think it's just a whim of his, this party of chairs. Rich people can afford to indulge their whims."

On our arrival that morning, Mandon had taken up a position on the top step between two brand-new concrete lions, couchant, with the raised mold seam still running down their backs. There was a pause, then Mandon seemed to swell up. He raised his head, spread his arms extravagantly and announced, "I Welcome you to Betton Place." We stood for a minute uncertainly in the gravel sweep, our bags slouched around our feet and our chairs stacked seat-to-seat behind us. Then we all crept into the entrance hall where we stood gazing at the coral- and chamois-colored walls and sneaking furtive glances into a black marble bathroom with gold-plated fixtures and a gilt mirror. Our bags were taken to our rooms on the second floor. Mandon energetically lined up our chairs in a neat row in the middle of the front room and then began to serve us an elaborate cream tea out of an elegant blue and gold Royal Crown Derby tea set.

Mandon was a perfect host, pouring out tea, passing slices of lemon, handing around a plate of little cakes, and getting the conversation started by introducing subjects of general interest. But his guests, in spite of the blood tie, were not congenial, and once begun, the conversation skewed off in odd directions.

Our cousin Bette, a plump fluffy woman from Arkansas, made herself a sandwich out of a scone, raspberry jam, and clotted cream, and told me all about her prize-winning chickens, Silver Laced Wyandottes and Buff Orpingtons. She had a way of catching her breath in little gasps and rushing on after each pause to prevent her listener from getting in a word that might divert the conversation from the subject of poultry. She was describing the symptoms of some of the most dreaded poultry diseases — premature molts and bloody droppings — but I found it hard to follow her because I was waiting for cream and jam to ooze out of her little sandwich and plop on the beige sculpted carpet.

On the other side of the row of chairs, Lance, a cousin who sold real estate in Colorado, was pouring rum into his tea and telling Lilly that this home on the Rappahannock reminded him of some really nice new homes he had recently sold in a waterfront development in Aspen.

"I don't disapprove of whimsy," Eleanor was saying to Bob, a cousin from Seattle who had painted red toenails on the ball-and-claw feet of his chair. Eleanor had an expressive way of drinking tea, taking a sip during a well-timed pause in her speaking then releasing her cup with a tiny toss so that it clinked into its saucer with an emphatic little tap. "I don't disapprove of whimsy" (pause, sip). "I just believe that whimsy has its place, and that place is NOT *(tap!)* on the ball-and-claw feet of an eighteenth-century Chippendale chair."

"Why do you call them homes if no one lives there?" Lilly asked Lance the real estate salesman.

"Coccidiosis," Bette concluded with a gasp and sank her teeth into her sandwich. Sure enough, there came the dollop of raspberry-stained cream. I dove in with a tiny lace napkin, but too late — *plop* — it hit the rug.

"Well, whatever resonates for you," Bob from Seattle told Eleanor, clutching his cup in both hands and ignoring the saucer.

"United by Our Chairs," pronounced Mandon, holding out his hands and smiling beatifically at us all. He had a way of stating pieces of sentences thoughtfully, with a ponderous emphasis, as if they were the titles of docudramas we might see one night on cable TV.

After tea we all went upstairs to unpack our things. My room was filled with exquisite furniture — a Sheraton mahogany canopy bed, a Queen Anne card table with a pie-crust edge, an eighteenth-century Philadelphia highboy, and a frail old pair of delicate Windsor chairs. But all the drawers were empty, the chairs stood in two dark corners of the room where no one would care to sit, and displayed on the card table was a horrifyingly fragile porcelain statue of two Carolina wrens on the branch of a flowering crab-apple tree. I held my breath and examined the exquisite little porcelain feathers and the pink and white porcelain crab-apple blossoms. The petals were as thin as real flower petals, and even down in the depths of each flower, beneath the cluster of threadlike porcelain stamens, there was not a speck of dust.

In the bathroom a light came on automatically when the door was opened, the toilet flushed with a silent slurp, and the mirror transformed itself into a TV screen with the touch of a button. But I was afraid to take a bath for fear I might splash water somewhere it didn't belong, and my orange "tartar control" toothbrush looked so odd on the parchment-colored Corian countertop that I d after that the conversation was left up us.

Lance began to bear down on Lilly, who ept taking little steps backward until she as pressed up against the row of chairs nd could retreat no farther. "But I dislike old weather," she said to him in a ringing one, "and I don't know how to ski."

Bob was describing the stages of his life to Eleanor, who was listening very attentively without understanding any of it. "I was in New York City — Greenwich Village — in the mid-sixties," he chanted, in a kind of rhythmic harangue, with drunkenly exaggerated dramatic pauses. "I was in the Bay Area — San Francisco — for the summer of love. . . ." He began to rock and sway. "I was at Woodstock in 1969. . . . I was in northern New Mexico '75 through '80. . . . I was in Seattle in '91."

"And now," Eleanor said brightly, falling under the spell and gesturing with her cup and saucer, "here you are in Virginia's northern neck on the banks of the Rappahannock in 1993."

Bette had fixed Mandon with her beady glare and was telling him about a special South American breed of chickens whose blue, green, and pink eggs were said to be low in cholesterol. "Araucana, a beautiful

34

stuffed it out of sight in the pocket of my terry-cloth robe.

In spite of the cold, Lilly and Eleanor and I went for a walk down the hill toward the river. At the end of the drive we stopped and looked up the avenue of shoulder-high Bradford pear trees to the house.

"It looks like a fungus," said Lilly.

"He wants our chairs," said Eleanor.

Supper that night was rather stiff and formal. Only Eleanor knew which pieces of silverware to use for each dish, and Bette spilled her wine. Afterward, coffee was served in the big room where we had had tea, and Mandon organized us into teams and partners to play word games, as a way of "getting to know each other," he said.

"As if he thinks we don't have sense enough simply to converse," Eleanor hissed under her breath.

Finally Mandon stood up and announced, "And now — " he paused dramatically, "Story Time."

"He means well," Eleanor whispered to me. "Poor thing, he just doesn't know any better."

"The Chairs Speak!" Mandon announced. He explained that he wanted each of us to tell one incident from the life of our chair. "It can be a story from the past or the

31

present," he said, "tragic or comic."

There was silence. We were thinking.

"Who will begin?" Mandon prompted.

Lance the real estate salesman stood up. He said that he would be "forever grateful to his chair, and — " he swept his arm out in an imitation of Mandon's welcoming gesture between the lions, "to Mandon, for giving all of us this super weekend in this super location."

There was a pause after that. Lilly winced, and Mandon gravely bowed his head in acknowledgment.

Then Bette flounced up and cleared her throat nervously. Her grandfather had died in her chair, she said, late one night. He had not been found until the next morning. ". . . Found dead, sitting bolt upright," she finished with a smack then flounced back down.

There was a moment of silence as everyone's eyes slid over to Bette's chair, an end chair, the mate to Lilly's. I pictured the dead man at the head of the table, leaning back gently against the carved splat in the early-morning light, his hands drooping peacefully over the arms.

Mandon went next. His was a perfect little story, with beginning, middle, and end, about the difficulties of choosing furniture

to ship to his summer cottage in M   ar
deciding to leave his pair of Chi   to
chairs here, in Virginia, because,
this was their home.   k

Then came Lilly's story, a sweet one   v
thing to do with cats.   a

Eleanor told about her grandfathe
used to sit on the porch in the chai
Pembroke table for whole summer d
a time, writing down his opinions w
quill pen.

Bob, from Seattle, told us that for
past ten years he had lived his life
spiritual plane, and that he had once ta
his chair way up into the red hills near Sed
and sat in the middle of an old Indian me
cine wheel, facing the sunrise.

I wasn't sure if these were the kinds
stories Mandon wanted to hear, and I brief
thought about making up something mor
dramatic, maybe of historical significance
Robert E. Lee sat in my chair for a haircut
before Appomattox. But in the end I told
the truth. I had once seen a lizard catch a
dragonfly on the seat of my chair. "He had
a little trouble with the wings," I mumbled,
"but in the end he managed to swallow the
whole thing."

Then Mandon made a speech about the
importance of family ties, coffee was served,

bird, no two alike, what we call multi-purpose, meaning good layers and a good meat bird. Good setters, too, although now, of course, we discourage that." She paused for breath, and Mandon made a gesture of withdrawal, but she gasped and rushed on: "Now, how many people do you know, Mandon, who can gather naturally colored Easter eggs in their baskets every day of the year?" But it was a rhetorical question, not requiring an answer, and Mandon, with an outstretched arm, turned to me.

"Will you come into my study?" he said. "I'd like to discuss something with you."

He sat behind a giant desk with a green leather top, and I perched on a stiff sofa covered with a kind of bristly fabric. He poured a few drops of Chambord into two big-bowled glasses, and we sat together in silence. I began to feel a kind of creeping claustrophobia, shut up with Mandon in that little room with its heavy woodwork, dark brocade draperies, and coffee-colored walls. I was relieved when he finally began to speak.

"The Chairs," he said. Then, with deep, reverential tones he began to talk about the value of our eight Chippendale chairs. As individuals, he explained, they were without significance, almost without worth. "But as a set," he said slowly, and he loomed across the desk at me, "as a set — they are priceless. And with your help," he went on, "with the help of each of you," he repeated, savoring his words, "I am in a position to reunite that set."

Then he began to talk about money. I don't know how long he talked. I felt dizzy, as if all the oxygen in the room had been displaced by the thick, sweet smell of raspberries, and the gold-leaf border above the picture molding seemed to twinkle rhythmically at me out of the shadows, and in the end I staggered joyfully out into the light and air.

That night I lay flat on my back in the Sheraton mahogany bed, staring up at the ecru lace canopy. I kept thinking about my old dinged-up Chippendale chair, with the rump-sprung, threadbare fabric seat I had tacked on it myself, in this house full of intimidatingly flawless furniture, and I couldn't sleep. Late in the night I got up and crept downstairs.

There in the front room were our chairs lined up in a straight row, just as Mandon had placed them. But in a chair near the middle of the row someone was sitting in the dark. A ghost, I thought, remembering Bette's grandfather "found dead." But when I went closer I could see that it was just

Eleanor, sitting in her chair, straight and still. Her wispy gray hair was loose, hanging down her back like cobwebs, and her hands were folded in her lap. She was just sitting there in the dark, staring at the wall.

The next day was our last at Mandon's estate on the Rappahannock. Breakfast was a quiet meal. There were no games, Lance had given up on luring Lilly to the slopes, Bob looked pasty and sick, and Bette was not talking about chickens.

After breakfast Mandon ushered us out the front door and down the lawn. It was warmer, the clouds were breaking up, and the ragged patches of snow were melting. And there, lined up on the grass, facing the river, were the chairs. We stood together in a little knot while Mandon strode down the hill with his camera and whirled around to face us, adjusting the lens.

"In position now," he called, and like so many trained rats we separated and took up our places, each behind his own chair for the last time.

"Smile!" called Mandon. And we did.

Red The Rat Man

One night I heard scampering and thumping in the walls. My first impulse was, Call Red The Rat Man. But Red The Rat Man has been dead for fifteen years. Besides, I remembered, toward the end he wouldn't kill rats anyway.

In his early years Red The Rat Man was a wizard exterminator. He knew and understood rats. "You got to know the mind of a rat," Red The Rat Man would say, tapping his own head. "The mind of a rat."

Then he would disappear under the house, dragging a jar of peanut butter, a roll of wire, and traps of all sizes. He didn't believe in rat poison. "The rats eat that poison, then they crawl into your walls and die. Stink up the place. Besides," he would add, turning away, "it's a suffering death, with poison. Traps kill 'em clean."

There would be some scuffling noises under

the house, and some snaps and clicks, and after a while he would crawl out, brush off his knees, and drive off in his rickety old pickup truck with "Red The Rat Man" stenciled on the door. For five years or more we would not see or hear a rat in our house.

Of all rats, Red The Rat Man admired pack rats the most. "They are the most intelligent of rats," he would tell us. When he found a pack rat nest under the house, he would make us all crawl under there with him to see it. It would be lined with soft fur and decorated with nandina berries. There would be shiny things glinting in the straw, and bright bits of fabric. "Red is the favorite color of the pack rat," Red The Rat Man would say.

On the rare occasions when he managed to catch a pack rat in a trap, he would make us all gather round. He would reverently lay the dead rat on its back and stroke its white belly. "See here," he would say, parting the rat's front legs, "Two little titties, right on her chest." And sure enough, there they would be, two pink nipples. "Onliest animals that have that is people, elephants, and pack rats." Red The Rat Man would hold the dead rat in his two hands and shake his head. "A noble rat," he would say. "The prince of rats."

There's something endearing about a man who loves rats, and women kept marrying Red The Rat Man. Each one thought she could cure him of his terrible alcoholism and turn him around. But as is so often the way, the thing that is the sweetest in the beginning is the very thing that rankles in the end; the wives were neglected and ignored while the rats held sway, and one after the other they left Red The Rat Man to his rats and his gin.

Years passed. Red The Rat Man's back became stooped, his hands shook, and his eyes were bleary. More and more often rats would reappear just days after his visit. "That Red The Rat Man's lost his touch," people began to say.

Then a new exterminator moved into our area. He wore a white uniform and carried a spray can of poison with a long wand. Pretty soon he began spreading stories about Red The Rat Man.

Everywhere Red The Rat Man had been, the new exterminator said, he was finding the same thing. All the traps were baited, but none of them was set. And beside every trap was a handful of strange-looking nuggets. "I thought they were rat poison at first," the new exterminator said. "But when I got out in the light, I saw that they were nothing but dried lima beans. Dried lima beans painted bright red with enamel paint.

"It was a great gift he had, Red The Rat Man, as an exterminator," the new rat man said. "Too bad he let his emotions get in the way."

Now the rats were back at my house, and they were driving me crazy. I suspected they were pack rats because they were too smart to get themselves caught in the traps I set for them. And we seemed to share the same taste in fashion. They stole my beaten silver bracelet from Spain, my scarab ring, and my silk twill scarf from the Metropolitan Museum of Art. They stole my narcissus bulbs that I had been so carefully forcing to bloom in January. They stole my shiny multicolored rocks I had brought all the way from the Snake River in Idaho.

I lay in my bed and listened all night long to the rats rattling the rocks and rolling the bulbs around in the wall behind my bed. I wrapped the pillow around my head. "Damn your nobility, damn your two titties, damn your elegant taste," I ranted. I didn't get much sleep.

Finally the night came when I couldn't stand it anymore. The moon was full and the rats were lively. They were playing ninepin with my narcissus bulbs. I hurled myself out of bed, charged out to the tool chest, and got a crowbar. I prized a batten off the wall behind my bed. From inside I heard scampering, then silence. I pulled a couple of nails and slid out a board. I shined my flashlight into the space.

There was a huge rat's nest. It was lined with soft fur and my fringed silk scarf. One crimson rose had been neatly excised from the scarf's design, and its red fibers were woven in with the fur. Strips of tinfoil glinted. My red and green and blue rocks with their veins of gold glowed in the light. There was my silver bracelet and my scarab ring. And my narcissus bulbs were artistically arranged in a kind of serpentine wall around the whole thing.

I put a finger into the nest. It was so soft I couldn't even tell I was touching anything. There was a baby rat. It was pink and its eyes weren't open. I parted its front legs and shined my light. Sure enough, two little titties.

Very gently I pulled out the silver bracelet. I was careful not to disturb anything else. Then I slid the board back in place. I nailed the batten back on top. My bed is on casters, and I rolled it across the room. From that distance the noise wouldn't seem so loud. I crawled under the covers and closed my eyes.

"For you, Red The Rat Man," I whispered.

I slept peacefully all night long. And in the morning when I went into the bathroom, there was a little pile of something beside my toothbrush. An offering. Seven dried lima beans, painted bright red.

A Hot Night in '31

It is a late summer afternoon in Thomasville, Georgia, The City of Roses. All the stores are closed and the citizens are shut up in their houses, prisoners of air conditioning. One homeless man stretches out beside the big white dog in the shade of a Bradford pear tree in front of CoCroft's Music Store, and in the municipal rose bed by City Hall, Mrs. Helgert picks roses.

Mrs. Helgert thinks that because she was the Rose Queen in 1931 she has a lifelong right to pick roses in the municipal rose beds. No other Rose Queens exercise that right, and so far Mrs. Helgert has gotten away with it. I was never Rose Queen, so I stand way back from the rose bed and take the roses as Mrs. Helgert hands them out to me.

"Don't worry," she reassures me, "I was Rose Queen in '31."

Finally she makes her way out of the rose bed. "Oh," she says, throwing her head back gracefully and opening her arms in an expansive gesture. Mrs. Helgert, in spite of her age, still has some lovely ways. After all, she was Rose Queen in '31. "Oh," she says, "just smell that rosy air."

The roses are the modern thornless kind, guaranteed to be in bloom until Christmas, and there is no rosy smell, but Mrs. Helgert tries to pretend that she is not losing her sense of smell along with her short-term memory, and I don't point out to her that the roses are unscented.

Mrs. Helgert picks her way carefully out of the rose bed, and I lay the roses in her arms. She cradles them like she might hold a newborn baby. "Now," she says, "home. Mr. Helgert will be wanting his supper."

Mr. Helgert has not wanted his supper since 1972 when he died of prostate cancer, but we head purposefully back to Mrs. Helgert's apartment. In the little kitchen she arranges the roses in a crystal vase and tells me about her high-school graduation night. The tables in the library were covered with bouquets of white flowers, bridal-wreath spiraea and abelia, one for each graduating girl, but because she was Rose Queen, the flowers in Mrs. Helgert's bouquet were all white roses.

"Hot?" Mrs. Helgert says to me. "Honey! That was a hot night." Mrs. Helgert's mother had been afraid people would be able to see through her white voile skirt, so she put a lamp on the floor behind Mrs. Helgert and kept adding on petticoats.

We sit down in Mrs. Helgert's living room and drink iced tea. Mrs. Helgert reclines languidly on her chaise longue and admires the vase of roses on the little table in front of the window. They are a bright orange edged with pink and yellow, and they look a little out of place in Mrs. Helgert's dim apartment.

"Mr. Helgert brought me those roses," she says. "You know, I was Rose Queen in '31. Hot? Honey! That was a hot night."

Except for an occasional little criminal foray out into the municipal rose beds, Mrs. Helgert would be content to stay in her apartment where Mr. Helgert's hat still hangs on a peg by the door, and Mr. Helgert's socks still lie paired up in the top left dresser drawer, but this evening I talk her into taking a stroll downtown to see a tiny park our city horticulturist made out of a rubble-filled alley.

Our city horticulturist used to garden for Willie Nelson, and he came down here with all kinds of exuberant gardening ideas involving everblooming exotics that attract swarms of butterflies and climb up ingenious trellises. Everywhere he finds a little bare scrap of ground he digs it up and plants lantana and alamanda.

Mrs. Helgert and I walk down the winding herringbone brick path and sit on a little bench and wait for the moonflowers to open.

"Mr. Helgert planted this garden," Mrs. Helgert tells me. But I explain again about the city horticulturist and the lantana and Willie Nelson. I sing a little snatch of "On the Road Again."

"Willie Nelson is a famous singer," I explain.

"Oh, Willie Nelson, of course," Mrs. Helgert bluffs, "a famous singer." And she starts in singing "Smoke Gets in Your Eyes."

I want the late summer light, the old brick walls, and the charming little flower garden to turn Mrs. Helgert's mind loose so it can wander lightly and peacefully. But she keeps settling back on Mr. Helgert's gardening and the hot night in '31 like a baby clutching a nub of carrot or a gummy zwieback cracker in a sticky little fist. I show her specimens of the more spectacular flowers, the creamy loblolly bay and the mandavilla with its waxy pink throat.

47

"Vulgar flowers," Mrs. Helgert says with distaste, and I remember the prim white bouquets of bridal-wreath spiraea and abelia on the library tables.

"Just between us," says Mrs. Helgert, "Mr. Helgert's taste does run to vulgar flowers."

On the way back to Mrs. Helgert's apartment we pass the bright orange roses in the municipal rose bed by City Hall.

"Oh," says Mrs. Helgert, "I'll pick some to take home to Mr. Helgert."

"But Mrs. Helgert," I say.

"Don't worry," she says, stepping into the rose bed. "I was Rose Queen in '31."

I stand outside the bed and take the roses one by one as she hands them out to me.

"Hot?" says Mrs. Helgert. "Honey! That was a hot night."

The Language of Flowers

Years ago I had a dear friend who married a man who was addicted to gardening. They were a perfect match. Joe had charm; Delia had money. She loved flowers, and he was a gardener. He moved into her beautiful house, and within a week he had the bulldozers and the Vermeer tree movers in to rearrange the topography as the first step in his gardening plan.

Joe was a brilliant gardener, and soon he had altered Delia's acreage, which had been pleasant enough in its neglected state, almost beyond recognition. Where there had been a few ancient camellias straggling down a ragged sloping lawn, now there were terraces with rock walls and herbaceous borders. The overgrown pecan orchard was pushed up, and in its place was a field of Japanese flowering almonds and drifts of daffodils. At the bottom of the garden, where there had been a bog and a thicket, there was now a sylvan glade with the graceful fronds of maidenhair fern drooping into a still, dark pool. There was the sound of water, gouts of sunlight in the shade, and beyond that, a bright meadow of wildflowers surrounded by a carefully ordered and calculated wilderness.

Joe felt that he had gotten a late start with this garden, so he pushed his plantings for maximum growth with tons of fertilizer. His relentless pest management program involved a complicated sprinkling system that would automatically apply pesticides and fungicides in the proper proportions exactly twenty-four hours before the first swarm of aphids hit the budding trees, or the first black spot appeared on a rose leaf.

After just five years of this vigorous encouragement, the garden achieved its mature beauty. The hybrid tea roses with their glossy, flawless foliage stood as tall and dense as a phalanx of soldiers and bloomed until midwinter. The river birch trees spread their silvery shade over the slate walkways. The great coral pink and sunny yellow lotus blossoms swayed on their tall stems above the pool. Plants that weren't even supposed to grow in south Georgia thrived under Joe's care, and horticulturists came from miles around to visit the garden and talk to Joe about his methods.

Then one spring Delia developed allergies. She broke out in great welts and rashes, she itched all over, she couldn't sleep. She thought she was allergic to her cosmetics, so she threw out all her creams and lotions and powders. Her wide, bald-looking eyes stared hopefully out of her pale face, but still she itched and couldn't sleep. Joe decided she was allergic to synthetic fibers, and he bought her all new, expensive clothes made out of Sea Island cotton, linen, and silk. But still she itched and coughed and sneezed. Her eyes watered and her throat hurt.

Then Joe started taking her to special clinics, and she began having all her extra organs removed, just in case. Finally, after the hysterectomy, there was nothing left to take out, and she settled down to a life of torment. Joe was sweet to her. He did everything he could to make her comfortable, and he surrounded her with beautiful things. Every day he brought armloads of flowers in to her, and the bright rooms of the house were filled with bowls of peonies, roses with three-foot stems, blue flag irises, and lilies.

After nearly a year the doctors finally found something. It was cancer. Before three months passed, Delia was on her deathbed. I went to see her, but she didn't recognize me and just kept tossing her head feebly and mumbling the names of flowers. On her last night, Joe said, she sat up in bed with staring eyes, clutched the covers to her neck, and cried out, "Roses!" Then she died.

Joe organized a beautiful private ceremony, and Delia was buried in his rose garden.

Sometimes I go and visit my old friend's grave. Joe doesn't like us to bring flowers from outside, because of the threat of introducing some deadly spore, so I stand empty-handed and admire the sweep and the colors and the forms of the garden. On spring days when the roses are in full bloom, the air is saturated with their color. But, I notice, from the trees and hedges and borders not one bird sings, and from the sylvan glade not one spring peeper can be heard, and from those roses, so tall and dense, just the faintest whiff of malathion rises on the breeze.

Blood and Water

My great-aunt El had disappeared and then turned up again twice before my mother and I finally decided it was time to get someone to look after her. The first time, she had taken off to the old sulphur springs in Panacea, Florida, to "take the waters." The sulphur baths hadn't been in use since the 1920s, but the pools were still there, choked with pickerelweed and eelgrass.

"Where did you stay?" we asked her.

"Why, in the hotel," she chirped.

My mother and I exchanged skeptical glances. "But that hotel has been gone for years, and the pools must be crawling with snakes. And nobody knew where you were, El. What if something had happened to you?"

But she had had enough of our questions and gave us an arch look. "I always hooted before I went in," she said.

The second time she disappeared, we found

her sleeping in the coach house in her back-yard. It was the ghosts, she told us. "I can't stand those munching sounds they make at night. They're up 'til all hours, sucking marrowbones and rattling the silverware." Eating sounds of all kinds irritated my aunt El. She had always been irritable, even in sanity, when she could look after herself. Now it was worse. We didn't know what we were going to do about her.

El came for lunch every Thursday. We always got out the linen napkins and the crystal glasses, and in the winter my mother would have camellias floating in a shallow dish in the middle of the table, because El had a taste for elegance. The winter light would come slanting through the windows onto the flowers, and El would hold her glass in the stream of light. "Water," she'd say. "Such a pretty thing."

One Thursday she came to lunch with a bloody, oozing scab on her shin. "El!" we exclaimed. "What happened?"

"Oh that," said El. "I sustained a slight injury from my fall."

"What fall?" asked my mother.

"It's those elephants. They come in all night long. In the front door, with their nasty trunks probing into everything, and I shoo them out the back. I assure you, Lila, not a wink of sleep do I get on those nights! Not a wink, my dear!"

My mother and I were very serious that Thursday afternoon. What should we do? We thought and thought. Finally Mama said firmly, "We'll just have to call Ralph."

Ralph was El's nephew, the son of her estranged sister, Rhoda. Rhoda and Ralph had lived together in Eufaula, Alabama, where they had run a boardinghouse. Rhoda had died a year or two ago, and we had heard that Ralph was at loose ends. We didn't hear these things from El. Because of a dispute over a silver tea service, El and Rhoda had been on the outs for thirty years. It was a subject we avoided, and except for occasionally muttering, "Rhoda can just keep her old tea pot!" El did not speak of Rhoda to us. But we now decided that since Ralph was, after all, El's own nephew, and we were related to her only through marriage, he should be notified about her condition.

"Blood is thicker than water," Mama reassured me.

When Ralph came, we knew we had done the right thing. He got off the bus, all smiles, dressed all in white, wearing a Panama hat and light tan perforated shoes. He was slew-footed and walked with an energetic lurch. Ralph was so thin that there was a question whether there was anything at all in his clothes. It was a relief when he sat down and we could see the outline of an angular knee pressed against his trousers.

"Now tell me all about Ellis," he said cozily. "You know I took care of Mother for years, God rest her soul. And she had her problems in the later years. Her memory, you know. It began to fail her." He gave us a look. "Now tell me all about Ellis."

We hesitated. Only Rhoda had called El "Ellis." Ralph seemed so good to us. But El was capable of holding a grudge for generations.

"Well, you know, Ralph, with El it's not so much her memory as it is . . . well, her disposition," Mama told him.

"Don't worry about a thing," Ralph told us generously. "I've had so much experience with these things. Just take me to her."

We took him to her. El eyed him suspiciously. We had told her that he was coming for a visit, that we were worried about her being alone in the house. She showed him to a little room off the kitchen porch. She had dragged a cot into the room and had thrown two sheets, a pillow, and a blanket on it. "Here's where you stay," she told him.

Ralph seemed very gracious and pleased,

and gave us a cheerful wink as we left him. "I'm used to this," he whispered conspiratorially. "Mother, you know."

Mama and I spent an uneasy night. We held ourselves away until eleven the next morning; then we drove to El's house. There was Ralph in his white clothes, all knob and shank. He had scrubbed the kitchen floor, cleaned the stove, and was sprinkling borax around the edges of the room. El was acting sullen, but at least she was home and not talking about elephants.

"He's after the roaches," she told us. "He's using the mass extinction approach." She sniffed. Her preferred method of dealing with roaches was to creep into the kitchen in the dark of night, suddenly switch on the light, and then fly into a wild stamping dance as the frantic roaches fled for their lives. Every time a roach would escape under the arch in front of her heel she'd say, "Drat!"

"Drat!" Stamp. Stamp. "Drat!" Stamp. "Drat!"

We preferred Ralph's way and told El so. We wanted to help him win her heart.

"Humph," she said. "He doesn't give the roaches a chance. At this rate there won't be a roach left in the house in a month."

We demurred. Ralph smiled brightly and moved into the pantry with the borax.

Things seemed to get better and better at El's house. The grass was mowed, the flower beds were weeded and edged. Ralph even tarred the roof gutters and fixed a leak by the chimney. El's clothes were always clean and pressed. She made no mention of ghosts, she had no more mysterious injuries, and we always knew that she was safe because Ralph drove her anywhere she wanted to go.

Ralph was paid a small salary through El's trust fund, and Mama negotiated with the bank to give him a raise. That Saturday when he called to give us the weekly report on El's condition and activities, he thanked Mama profusely and said that he was perfectly able to live on his original salary and was arranging an automatic monthly deduction at the bank to have the extra money donated to the Heart Fund. That Ralph! We shook our heads.

At Christmas we planned an extra fancy dinner for El and Ralph: roast pork, mashed potatoes, the usual vegetable casseroles and souffles, and a fragrant loaf of yeast bread that had risen so magnificently over the edges of the pan that it had great golden crusty shoulders. For dessert we had made Old English Fruit Trifle in a crystal bowl so that every layer shone gemlike through the faceted glass.

Ralph ate some of the pork stuffing, no pork, a small serving of each of the vegetables, and no bread.

"I never eat bread unless it's whole wheat," he said with a sigh.

But when he saw the trifle he lit up. His clothes began to shiver around his bones. "Trifle!" he said reverently. We were surprised. We'd never heard of Old English Fruit Trifle until we found a recipe in the cookbook as we were looking for something extra fancy and delicious. We were delighted that we had one thing for Christmas dinner that Ralph would relish.

"It's the most elegant and sumptuous of all desserts. That cream!" he gushed.

We smiled. This was the joy of cooking! Mama served Ralph an enormous dollop and gave him an extra scoop of clotted cream.

But Ralph held up his hand. "None for me, thank you," he said, tapping his teeth with a fingernail. "My teeth, you know. All that sugar." Then he added brightly, "I'll enjoy seeing you eat it, though." I choked on the apricot layer. Mama said she'd prefer to have her trifle later in the afternoon. El wolfed hers down, then ate the one Mama had served for Ralph.

"There's nothing wrong with his teeth," she snarled through the cream. "He's out there in his room 'til all hours, crunching away. I can hear it through the walls." Ralph beamed at her.

When they had gone, Mama said, "I'm worried about Ralph. He shouldn't have to put up with El's treating him this way. I'm going to have to have a little talk with him."

The next day she asked Ralph to come over. She had herb tea (no caffeine) and little dry squares of whole wheat toast. We sat in the front room, and she poured out tea.

"Ralph," she said, "we're worried about you. You're working much too hard, and you're letting El be mean to you."

Ralph began his protest. "But I don't mind, Lila, really I don't. I'm used to it. Mother, you know."

But Mama was ready for him. "I know you don't mind, Ralph. I know you're used to it. But you should mind. And you shouldn't be used to it. Ralph," she said, "you need to have some fun."

"But," said Ralph, "I enjoy — "

"No, Ralph," Mama said. "I want you to take El's car tonight and go to the movies. Don't worry about El. Go to the grocery store and buy yourself a candy bar. Get a good book to read. Sleep late in the morning."

There was a long silence. Ralph stood up. He touched each corner of his mouth with the edge of his napkin then folded it in the original creases and laid it on the tea tray. "I'll think about what you said, Lila."

"I want you to, Ralph."

"I will think about it," said Ralph. And then he was gone. We agreed that he had taken it very well. We couldn't wait to see if there would be results.

One day about a week after the little talk, Mama came in looking distracted. "I saw the strangest thing downtown. A man sitting on the curb on Baldwin Avenue with his feet in the gutter. He had his britches rolled up to his thighs, and he was drinking beer from a quart bottle through a soda straw." She paused. "He had the longest, whitest legs." She put down a sack of groceries and turned to me. "I think it was Ralph."

We called El's house. She answered the telephone. No, Ralph hadn't been there for several days. She didn't know where he had gone. He had taken her car.

We went right over. El was in the kitchen, sweeping borax into a dustpan. She straightened up when she saw us coming.

"Ralph's off his rocker," she told us. "He came in here one afternoon last week with that hat on his head. He ate all the shortbread, see?" She thrust the empty tin under our noses. With solemn faces we peered inside. Sure enough, only crumbs and pleated papers. We looked at each other. We nodded thoughtfully. El was right. Ralph was off his rocker.

Mama and I decided to spend the night at El's house, just in case Ralph returned after dark on a mad rampage. We had heard of such things happening. Mama lay down on the sofa in the living room. I tried to sleep in the spare bedroom. The house was still. The roaches had not returned. I lay on the bed with my eyes pressed wide against the dark. Somehow, the thought of Ralph eating shortbread and drinking beer through a soda straw was much more frightening than the nocturnal elephants and gluttonous ghosts of El's demented fantasies.

I heard Mama rustling the sofa cushions in the living room.

"Mama, are you asleep?" I whispered.

"Certainly not," she replied. It was some comfort.

We lay there in El's house and waited. We could hear a steady and sonorous snore from El's bedroom at the back of the house.

Finally, at about two o'clock in the morning we heard the car drive in. We popped up and dashed to the window. Through a

chink in the shutter slats we saw Ralph, gleaming in his white clothes, reel out of the car and up the front walk. He was barefooted. His tan perforated shoes were tied together by the shoestrings and looped around his neck. I couldn't take my eyes off his strange, wraithlike feet. I'd never seen feet so white, so long, so stringy. They were the kind of feet that should not be seen. He was holding something pinched between the finger and thumb of each hand and couldn't open the door. We let him in. Mama's eyes were wide. Mine felt as if they had not blinked for hours. There was Ralph in his Panama hat.

"Bailey! Lila!" he sang out. "I'm delighted to see you! Just delighted, I'm sure!" He sprawled on the sofa, legs flailing. Then in a flash he drew himself up tight, clamped his knees together, pursed his lips, and offered us each a date stuffed with cream cheese. "One for you, and one for you."

We gingerly held out our hands. The stuffed dates looked like plump roaches. We had not said a word to Ralph. Finally Mama started up.

"Ralph," she said, "don't you think you'd better go to bed? We'll talk about . . ." She looked at the date in her hand, then at Ralph's feet. ". . . all this tomorrow."

"To bed? My dear Lila, I should say not! I'm going on a trip. Just stopped by to collect my things. I've discovered the most amazing airline, run by Trappist monks out of the mountains of north Georgia. They're coming to pick me up at 2:33 A.M., just a few seconds from now it seems, so if you'll just eat those dates, I'll say good-bye and be off."

"But Ralph," Mama began. She'd been looking after people all her life, but this was beyond her range of experience.

Just then we heard a bustling from down the hall. And here came El. Her white hair was standing wildly up on her head, and she was wearing a siren-red nylon nightgown that stopped at the floor in a full ruffle.

"Ralph!" she said fiercely. And she looked fierce, too. Her eyes were sparkling. "Where have you been? And don't start in telling me about those crazy Trappist air pilots. They're not to be trusted. Look at you, Ralph."

We all looked at Ralph. He must have been wearing those same white clothes for a week. All his bones showed through. Three buttons were missing from his shirt.

Ralph looked down at himself. He stuck out one foot and wiggled the toes. He stuck out the other foot. He looked at El.

"You're right, Ellis. I'm not myself," he said.

"And a good thing too!" El crowed. Then she took him by the arm and hauled him into his room by the kitchen porch. She tightened the sheets on his little bed. She brought him a glass of water. She took his hat off his head and laid it carefully on the chair by the bed. She gave him a pat. She gave the hat a pat.

"Sweet dreams!" she chirped. "Tomorrow we'll eat the crystalized ginger, Ralph!"

Then she flitted off down the hall to her bedroom. The ruffle of her nightgown followed her in a mad wake. We heard the bed springs sigh as Ralph lay down. Then not a sound.

Mama and I looked at each other. We looked at the sweating dates in our hands. We tiptoed out, quietly closed the door behind us, and made our way through the shadowy bushes. Everything was dewy and peaceful and quiet. Even the night sounds had stilled. Mama tossed her date into the shrubbery, and we got into the car.

"Blood is thicker than water," she said. And we drove away from that sleeping house.

Mr. Bonzonio

I was typing along the other day when suddenly I heard a snap, then a hissing snakelike sound, and then a little dirty-looking piece of leather fell out of the back of the typewriter, and everything went limp. I had to take the typewriter in to Mr. Bonzonio, who runs an office equipment and repair store downtown.

In a little flurry of marketing zeal back in the 1950s, Mr. Bonzonio had arranged a complete office setup in his store window: a green metal desk with rounded steel edges, a black plastic swivel chair on casters, a great gray beast of an electric typewriter, a black adding machine with a crank on the side you snatch down to print your numbers on the tape, a rectangular black metal trash can, and the kind of calendar with the metal hoops and a page for every day of 1955. Over the years a layer of dust has settled over everything, and dust fuzz has piled up in the corners of the window like dingy snow.

Somewhere in the back of the store, among the towering stacks of office machines and office furniture and obsolete office gadgets, Mr. Bonzonio himself crouches in front of a little black-and-white television set with the volume turned up high, the Miss Havisham of clerical merchandise. I stagger through the maze with my typewriter, in and out around a stack of ten gross adding-machine tapes teetering on top of a glass display case of dusty fountain pens and dried-up magic markers. In the outer layers of the clutter are newer machines — Brother typewriters and big clunky late-model IBMs. But deeper in the pile the machines are older, and stacked against the wall are the real antiques — gorgeous old Underwood uprights with gold fleur-de-lis, the gleam of nickel plating, and delicate little gears and levers all exposed in the back.

I follow the sound of daytime drama until I find Mr. Bonzonio at the very back of the store. I shove aside a pile of dehydrated red and black typewriter ribbons and set my machine down with a clunk. I show him the shred of leather and demonstrate the limp carriage.

"Drawbar," snaps Mr. Bonzonio. He turns

back to the television. "Come back tomorrow."

But I feel an attachment to my old typewriter. "I don't want to leave it here . . ." I gaze around the store at the shelves and shelves of springs and gears and sprockets and gutted typewriters and reams of yellowing paper and uncoiling rolls of adding-machine tape and balls of dust the size of newborn babies. ". . . overnight."

Mr. Bonzonio sighs. He roots around in a deep drawer and comes out with a bright, brand-new–looking leather strap. Both his hands disappear in the back of my typewriter. I hear some whirring and clicking; then Mr. Bonzonio hurls the carriage to the right, glides it to the left, and whacks the space bar a few times with his big flat thumb. The bell dings, and he says, "That'll be five ninety-five, and you'll have to carry it out yourself. I'm eighty-nine years old. No deliveries and no heavy lifting."

He turns back to the television, and I stagger with my typewriter down the narrow path between the towers of office supplies. As I struggle to open the door, Mr. Bonzonio shouts after me, "And I've quit taking inventory!"

Rocks

My Aunt Belle loves rocks. Her whole house used to be filled with rocks. Every flat surface was covered with slabs of amethyst crystal, piles of rainbow-colored labradorite, bowls full of fossilized sharks' teeth as big as a child's hand, and agate geodes lined with quartz crystals. Outside, bigger, rougher rocks were piled up to the eaves, with scant little chinks left for doorways and windows.

Every afternoon my aunt Belle takes a bagful of rocks down to Shoney's restaurant where she spreads them out on the Formica tabletop and says incantations over them while she drinks iced tea. Long before it became fashionable, she was a believer in the healing powers of rocks, and any member of the family who fell ill could expect it: one day, a tiny brown paper package would arrive by mail, and inside, nestled in tissue paper, would be a little polished pink or green or brown stone.

Aunt Belle loves her rocks, and for many years she did not bestow them lightly. She would wait until the symptoms had increased and the case was declared hopeless. There William would lie gasping on his deathbed. His wife opens the package with trembling hands. There's the rustle of tissue paper, then a moment of silence. "Belle has sent William a healing rock," she murmurs.

"Oh my dear," her friend commiserates, pulling on her coat and heading out the door to bake a ham, "it won't be long now."

Every summer I go to visit Aunt Belle and we go on rock-hunting expeditions. But Aunt Belle has slowed down in recent years, and now she spends less time on the trail of rocks and more time sitting in Shoney's restaurant admiring her collection and imbuing each rock with special powers. She likes the way the sun shining in the west windows at Shoney's seems to light the rocks up from the inside, and she likes the air conditioning on summer afternoons.

And as she grows older, Aunt Belle has begun to give her rocks away more easily. Now we get rocks when we have indigestion or a sprained wrist. It took some getting used to. Many a family member suffering from a slight cold, on finding a rock from

70

Belle in the mail, went scurrying to the *Complete Medical Guide* to read up on typhoid fever, diphtheria, and cholera. But we have gotten used to it now and think nothing of it when we receive rocks even for Christmas presents and birthdays.

Now more and more it seems Aunt Belle herself is ailing. I remember the days when she could walk six miles down Mogarts Beach and six miles back, carrying a five-gallon bucket full of rocks and fossil seashells in each hand, and sit up all night studying the surfaces of each one through her loupe. Now she sometimes needs help stepping up on the curb at Shoney's, and she takes a nap every afternoon. And her rock collection is dwindling. In her house doors can be opened and closed without banging into rocks, and the tops of tables and dressers, once home to desert roses, geodes, thunder eggs, and ruffled oysters, are now bare.

I can imagine a summer, not too long from now, when I'll go to visit Aunt Belle in a house I've never seen, with empty windowsills and broad sweeps of bare floor. Aunt Belle won't feel like driving to Mogarts Beach to look for quartz crystals formed a million years ago in the mouths of fossilized clamshells. She won't even feel like going to Shoney's to drink iced tea. And while she takes a nap upstairs, I'll wander around the house looking through the empty drawers of the old scraped and dented furniture and peering under sofas and behind cabinets at the scarred, gouged floor. But in that whole house there will not be a single healing rock to be found.

Folk Art

"I think this is the road," Ms. Hamilton said. "I remember that shed with the corrugated metal siding. But I thought it was on the other side of the road."

My cousin Lilly and I were on an excursion with a group of teachers for a summer class we were taking: The Arts in the Classroom. The instructor, Ms. Hamilton, had come down from Atlanta to teach us about art. During the first week we had made "junk art" using buttons, scraps of fabric, paper clips, and lots of glue, and learned some interesting facts about Indian lore. This week we were on "folk art." We'd seen a video of a wild-eyed man explaining in a high-pitched voice how God spoke to him.

"God speaks in mysterious ways," he keened. "Can't just anybody understand him. You got to have the knack. Now, me," he said, his eyes blazing, "I got the knack. I've knowed just a couple of other people in my life had the knack."

The camera zoomed in on an example of his artwork. It looked like chunks of firewood nailed together. It stood on four rickety legs in a weedy yard. We squinted our eyes. Was it an antelope? A muskrat? The camera focused on his face as he spoke.

"All a this," he said, gesturing grandly, "all a this here is God's work."

We could see that his yard was filled with firewood gargoyles. Some had pieces of sheet metal tacked onto them. Some were hanging from trees by ropes and cables. In the background a mangy-looking dog raised its leg on the firewood muskrat.

Then the film showed another folk artist, a neatly dressed man who made tiny wood carvings, incredibly realistic. "The world is really this size," he said. "It just seems big to us because we live in it. But there are just a few, sir, a privileged few, to whom God shows the world as he made it. Now me, sir, I am one of those few." The camera lingered on his face as he pursed his lips and nodded emphatically. His eyes flickered wildly from left to right. Then we saw his life's work on a card table. It was an entire village, carved out of wood, four feet square. There were houses with people inside, trees, fences, tiny trains and cars with wheels that moved. It was cute. But I wasn't sure I understood folk art.

Today we were going on a field trip in the northwest part of the county, out old Dollar Store Road, to see our own local folk artist, Mary Lawrence Shepard. Lilly and I had never heard of her. Ms. Hamilton, who was a great student of folk art, was driving us in the school van. We were lost.

"That trailer should be on the left. We're going the wrong way!" Ms. Hamilton announced. We turned around, and after a few miles, an old building loomed into view. The siding was falling off, and the roof was caved in. Two mattresses had been thrown out on the ground, and their stuffing was clinging to briar bushes like cotton bolls.

"That's the store," said Ms. Hamilton. "Her house is next."

We parked on the side of the road and all climbed out. We were used to the air-conditioning of the van and felt stupefied by the sudden heat. The sun was dazzling. We stood on the side of the road and fanned ourselves. Gnats the size of horseflies buzzed around our ears. One of the teachers discovered she was standing in a fire-ant bed.

"I'll see if she's home," Ms. Hamilton said, and she headed down a little dirt path.

Through the bushes we could see parts of a house.

"At least it'll be shady in there," said Lilly, peering into the leaves.

After a few minutes Ms. Hamilton came back and led us down the path. We walked under a wisteria trellis, through an arched gateway in a rough plastered concrete wall, and into Mrs. Shepard's sculpture garden. Mrs. Shepard herself came down the steps of her porch to meet us. She was a tiny woman, over ninety years old, with wisps of white hair not quite covering her scalp, which showed through in patches as shiny and pink as stretched silk satin.

"I've brought these women out to see you, Mrs. Shepard," Ms. Hamilton said in a loud voice. "They are interested in your artwork."

Mrs. Shepard eyed us all brightly.

"They have come to see your artwork," Ms. Hamilton shouted.

"Well, they're welcome to look all they want," said Mrs. Shepard. "Course, a lot of it's broke down now, over the years," and she peered into the bright sunny yard beyond the wisteria shade. We could see dozens of concrete statues, blazing white in the sun, some covered with vines, some missing arms and heads, some crumbled into heaps of concrete chunks and twisted wire.

"Y'all go look at 'em. Make yourselves at home. You're welcome to stay as long as you like," said Mrs. Shepard. Then she turned and wafted back into her house.

We scattered over the yard like so many giant, brightly colored chickens. Ms. Hamilton had given us a printed guide to refer to, and Lilly and I began trying to find the statues on the list.

"This must be Red Cross Nurse," said Lilly. A headless concrete woman lifted a concrete veil to reveal a marble slab on which were carved all the names of Thomas County boys killed in World War I. The veil drooped in strangely graceful folds of chunky concrete. The nurse's feet, sensibly shod, toed in ever so slightly. "She looks like a good nurse," said Lilly, standing back and squinting in the sun.

Next we found a bust of Martha Berry, founder of Berry College. ONE OF THE GREATEST WOMEN IN GEORGIA was gouged out of concrete in fanciful script. Martha Berry's head was cocked to one side, and she had a coy little smile on her concrete lips. Her eyes were twinkling. "Cement and sand," Lilly read from the guide. "I wonder how she did it?"

After a while all the students gathered

under the wisteria canopy to hear Ms. Hamilton interview Mrs. Shepard.

She spoke confidentially into the microphone of a portable tape recorder. "This is Barbara Hamilton, July 21, 1989, at the home of Mary Lawrence Shepard, Thomas County, Georgia." Then she raised her voice. "Mrs. Shepard, when did you begin your work here?"

"1917," piped Mrs. Shepard promptly.

"And what was your inspiration?"

Mrs. Shepard stared at her.

"What made you do it? Where did you get the idea?" Ms. Hamilton persisted.

"Well, back in 1917 I saw in the paper where a club in Atlanta was going to raise a statue to the boys who fought so bravely in the war. They had to buy the land and pay somebody to do the sculpturing. The thought came to me that I had the land, didn't have to buy it, and I wanted to build something for our boys too. So I got started."

Ms. Hamilton probed for something less specific. "Mrs. Shepard, a lot of artists like you say that God speaks to them. They say that he tells them what to do. Their art is an expression of God through their hands."

Ms. Shepard stared at her. Her eyes looked huge behind her bifocal lenses. She blinked. It seemed like slow motion. Her eyelids swept down over her eyes and swept back up again. But nothing could stop Ms. Hamilton.

"Mrs. Shepard, do you feel that God is working through you when you make your statues?"

"Naw," said Mrs. Shepard. "Naw, I don't feel nothing like that."

There were a few more questions. Then we got into the van and drove back to town. The air-conditioning felt good.

"At least she's not crazy like those other folk artists," someone said. Then everyone began giving advice to the teacher who had stepped in the fire ants. Little red bumps had formed.

"It's too late for aloe."

"Absorbine Jr. will stop them from festering."

"Just don't pick at them!"

That evening our class attended an event of artistic importance in town. A heron or crane had been made out of solid bronze by an artist commissioned by the cultural society. Photographs from the 1870s showed such a bird on the courthouse fountain, but sometime during the 1920s it had disappeared. For over a year now, fashionable fund-raising events and drives had been sponsored by local heritage preservation organizations and arts guilds. "Bring Back the Bird!" had been their slogan. The $10,000 that was raised had gone to commission a well-known artist to do the sculpture. On this day the bird, fastened in place and plumbed to spray a jet of water from its beak, was to be unveiled.

"We are honored today," intoned Margaret Mires, president of Heritage, Inc., "to have with us Mr. Brice Clune. We were very fortunate that Mr. Clune accepted our offer to restore our fountain." Everyone clapped. Mr. Clune smiled. "We are honored to have the work of an artist of Mr. Clune's standing in the heart of our town," continued Mrs. Mires. "And now, I know what you have all come to see, so without further ado — THE BIRD!" She smiled radiantly and gestured to the fountain.

By careful prearrangement and split-second timing, the water was turned on at the very instant the green velvet shroud was whisked from the statue. Water squirted, Mr. Clune smiled, and we all clapped. "Bravo!" someone shouted. "Bravo!"

The bird stood on the top of its pedestal, wings spread in tortured symmetry, neck stretched to the sky. The water spewed brokenly from its beak. One thin stream skeeted high into the air, another was diverted by an irregularity in the casting into a fan spray, and the rest burbled up an inch or two then splattered into the pool, drenching the bird. Its naked spraddle legs, sticking out of the meticulously wrought feathers, looked strangely indecent. I had to turn away.

"Do you think it's supposed to look like that?" I whispered to Lilly.

"He certainly seems proud of it," she whispered back. Brice Clune stood with his arms folded, his eyes fixed on the bird.

"The Artist and His Work," Lilly whispered. We giggled.

Then the group broke up, people crowded around Mr. Clune, and we could hear the murmur of congratulations, squeals of appreciation, and the unmistakable rustle of real silk.

Lilly and I drove to Burger King for some iced tea. It was late in the evening. The sun was going down.

"Let's drive out to Mrs. Shepard's place," Lilly said. "I'd like to see those statues again, now that it's not so hot."

When we got there, Mrs. Shepard met us on the porch. "You're some of them girls was out here today," she said, eyeing us cautiously.

Lilly explained how it had been so hot and bright then, and how we wanted to see

81

the statues again in the cool of the evening.

"Will you walk with us?" I asked.

"Well, it's rough ground out there," said Mrs. Shepard. "I mean it's rough for me. I'm an old woman now, see," she explained. "But, yeah, sure, I'll take a little turn with y'all."

A breeze had picked up. The air was cool, and the green of the grass, the trees, and the bushes gave the air an eerie green glow.

It was easier to look at the statues now. The shadows on the faces of the ones that still had their heads gave them more expression than they had had at noontime. Every one looked just right. We went back to Red Cross Nurse.

"This is my favorite," said Lilly. "You really did a good job on this one."

"Yep, she's a right nice one," said Mrs. Shepard. I was holding her arm, and I could feel her skin slipping over tiny sharp bones. "But I tell you, my best one's over yonder," she said.

We looked around.

"Honeysuckle got it," said Mrs. Shepard. "If you help me pull it off, I'll show you."

In the shade of an umbrella chinaberry tree we could see a mound of honeysuckle. "In here?" Lilly said.

"Yep," said Mrs. Shepard. "You pull that

honeysuckle off, you'll see her."

It was hard work. By the time we knew we were actually uncovering something it was nearly dark, and we finished in moonlight. We stood back to look.

The statue was of a woman, sitting on the cement edge of a pool. Her head was lowered and her eyes were looking down. There was no twinkle in her eyes and no coy smile on her lips. Her shoulders drooped, and her hands lay limp in her lap. Her feet in their cement shoes were the saddest feet I had ever seen. We stood back and looked at the statue in the moonlight. Lilly still held a sprig of honeysuckle in one hand.

"So sad," she whispered.

Then Mrs. Shepard said, "I told a lie today." A thin string of drool turned loose from the corner of her mouth. "Yes ma'am, I told a lie today."

We waited.

"He's in on it all right," she whispered. "Him and me, we worked together all them years back."

Then she started to climb down into the pool. I remembered the feel of her little frail birdy arm and made a move to steady her, but she was already on her hands and knees in the slurry at the bottom of the pool, rooting around and hurling gobs of wet leaves and scum over her shoulder. Lilly and I stood back.

"This thing's piped for water," Mrs. Shepard said. "Got to poke it out, make it skeet straight."

We could barely see her for the flying blobs of trash, but finally she climbed out, covered with mud and slime. Her glasses had been flung off somewhere, and her eyes were wide and bright. She stood back and stared at the statue and the pool.

"Turn it on! Turn it on!" she said, and in the tangle of honeysuckle at the foot of the chinaberry tree, Lilly found a valve. A jet of water rose into the sky, arched smoothly, then sobbed magnificently into the pool. We stood and watched it for a long time. The moonlight and the mist from the splashing water gave everything a strange luminescence.

"Yes, damn it," Mrs. Shepard whispered, "God's in on it all right. He talked to me in the night. He told me what to do, and I did it. I sure did. I filled up this yard with His work!" She was looking up at the sky, but with her hands she began gathering up her skirt and wringing it out, first one way, then the other. "Goddamn you!" she shouted up at the moon. "Goddamn you!" Her hands picked their way over to another section of skirt, gathered it up and began wringing and wringing.

"I did it all for you, and you left me, you left me with it! Speak up!" she yelled. She was crouched over now, with her skirt all pulled into a knot, looking up over her shoulder at the moon. "Speak to me! You don't speak to me no more!"

Lilly and I got her by her arms and led her into the house. We sat her on a sofa, and Lilly loosened her fingers one at a time and then held both her hands while I found a telephone number. Mrs. Shepard's daughter answered.

"She been talking to them statues again? Harold, it's a lady says Mama's been talking to them damn statues again. You got to take the tractor over there first thing. Thank you, ma'am, for calling. I'll be out there to take care of her directly. It's these moonshiny nights she takes on this a way. Gets out there with them statues, she gets plumb crazy. Harold's gon' bring the tractor over tomorrow and knock down ever' one of 'em. It's them statues is gon' be the death of Mama."

Lilly and I didn't say much on the way back to town. That strange light of Mrs. Shepard's garden, a combination of the green of dusk and the mist of the fountain was gone, and the fields and woods we passed shone almost garishly in the light of the moon. In the distance we could hear a faint rumble of thunder.

Native Air

People in the eighteenth century were great believers in the benefits of one's native air. The Campbells hoped that breathing the air of her birthplace for a year would bring Miss Jane Fairfax out from under her peculiar malaise, and one draught of her native air was sure to have cured Marianne Dashwood of her deadly putrid fever. But my native air — in the summertime a combination of heat and damp and green — is like air that has already been breathed.

In south Georgia in July there's no color but green. Anything that doesn't move sprouts a blanket of moss, and after every rain a green mist hangs in the air. The hydrangea bushes around my house grow up taller and taller until they spread their giant leaves against the windows, and the sunlight shining in is tinted green, and all the shadows have the shapes of leaves.

There is no distance in the color green, and a few weeks into July I feel as if I'm being smothered by verdure. That's when I get on a train and ride as far away from my native air as that train will go. I ride north until I don't know the names of the trees, and the birds sing out of tune, and in the afternoon there's a definite shade of blue in the haze.

Vegetation up north does not take over houses, and color the air, and break the bones of little old ladies in their own back-yards. Like a well-trained pet, it respects its borders and sits, stays, and heels on command. The shade up north is cool, the sun shines lightly, and from a distance a great dark forest looks like a little toy thing that a child might rearrange in an idle moment, and the hayfield tucked up neatly into one edge of it might be laid down and smoothed with two fingers.

But I can't stay gone forever. In the middle of August I get back on the train. It's late afternoon when I step off in Georgia. A light rain hovers in the air. The heat has melted the sap in the pine trees, and the dampness carries that bright smell. That night I lie in my own bed, so glad to be off that train. I breathe in a draught of my native air, so damp and green I can feel it coating my lungs, and, I realize, they were right in the eighteenth century — it's like a tonic. The weariness of travel seeps out of my bones, and as I fall asleep all the green things press against the screen. "Welcome home," they say.

SCENIC OVERLOOKS

Forbidden Things

I was leaning over the little railing, looking down into the Devil's Millhopper, an interesting geological formation and the focal point of a Florida state park. Waterfalls plunge 120 feet down into a bowl-shaped sinkhole; maidenhair ferns and moss grow in little crevices along the steep, sloping sides of the gorge; and a beautiful mist rises up.

I stood there, gazing down, and feeling a reverence for these spectacles of the natural world. I felt the slow sweep of geologic time. I felt the remnants of the spiritual significance this place had had for the Indians who lived here for thousands of years. I felt the wonder and awe of the first European explorers of Florida looking down into this chasm for the first time.

Then another feeling crept over me, a deep, almost atavistic longing. It was the urge to throw something down into the Devil's

Millhopper. I looked around. A stone or a stick would do, but what I really wanted was a piece of food, the nibbled end of a hotdog bun or a wedge of chocolate cake without the icing. Then I noticed the sign, one of those tastefully unobtrusive state park signs:

DO NOT THROW FOOD OR TRASH IN GORGE

It was 4:00 A.M. I was at the Los Angeles, California, bus station, my next-to-last stop on a dreary transcontinental bus trip — three days and three nights on a Greyhound bus. My back ached, my knees ached, my head ached. Ever since El Paso, Texas, my seatmate had been an old man who chain-smoked Marlboro cigarettes and sucked and slobbered over a perpetual ham sandwich that kept oozing out of a greasy crumple of waxed paper.

I longed for a bath in my own bathtub, and then a deep sleep in my own bed, stretched out full-length between clean sheets. But, I thought, pushing open the door of the bus station bathroom, if I just wash my feet and my hair I will be all right. I lined up my soap, my washrag, and my little bottle of shampoo on the back of the sink and took off my shoes and socks. Ahh, I thought. Then I saw the sign on the mirror:

DO NOT WASH HAIR OR FEET IN SINK

A few weeks ago I went into our little downtown restaurant and saw that it had replaced its tired old salad bar with a gorgeous saltwater aquarium with sea anemones, chunks of living coral, and big slow-moving colorful fish with faces I could almost recognize. I spent my whole lunchtime staring into that tank, mesmerized by the fish as they gracefully looped and glided, sending the tentacles of the sea anemones into slow twirls and fanning out the tall grasses.

When I finished my sandwich I noticed that there were a couple of crumbs left on my plate, just the size to pinch between thumb and finger. Oh, I thought, to pinch up those crumbs and dip my fingers down into the water, breaking through the smooth surface into the coolness and silence of that peaceful world. One of the fish would make a looping turn, his odd exophthalmic eyes would rotate slowly in their sockets and fix upon the crumbs in my fingers. Then he would angle up, and I would feel for just one exquisite instant those thorny fish lips rasping across my fingertips. With rising delight and anticipation, I pinched up a crumb, two crumbs. I scrabbled across the plastic top of the tank, found the little door, lifted it open — and then I saw the sign:

DO NOT FEED THE FISH
★ ★ ★
WE PROHIBIT CLIMBING IN ANY MANNER
FROM OR ALONG THE CANYON RIM
DO NOT PICK FLOWERS
NO SMOKING EATING OR DRINKING
NO SWINGING FROM VINES IN TREES
NO PEDESTRIAN TRAFFIC IN WOODS
NO FISHING
NO SWIMMING
NO TRESPASSING

Don't get me wrong; I approve of these prohibitions. Imagine the nasty mess in the bottom of the Devil's Millhopper if every self-indulgent tourist threw a piece of food into the sinkhole. Imagine the puddles on the floor and the plumbing complications in the Los Angeles bus station if every weary transcontinental traveler washed her hair and feet in the sink. Imagine the deadly scum of grease on the surface of that saltwater aquarium if every fish-dazed diner fed the catalufa his last mayonnaise-coated crumbs.

But sometimes I wonder: Who makes up these necessary and useful rules, and how does he know so well the deep and touching urges of human beings to pick flowers, walk in the woods, climb canyon walls, swing from vines, and feed already well-nourished animals? I imagine with distaste a mean, sour, silent little man skulking around in public places, watching us furtively with squinny eyes while scribbling notes on his pad with a gnawed pencil. In national parks he disguises himself as a tourist in reflective sunglasses and plaid Bermuda shorts. "Bryce Canyon," he notes with a smirk, "Urinating on hoodoos and off cliffs." In zoos he wears khaki and lurks in the shadows, hiding behind a bag of peanuts. "Touching giraffe's tongue through fence wire. . . . Feeling camel's hump," he scribbles.

At night he goes home, and in his stark white workshop, illuminated with fluorescent lights, he makes those signs. Rounded letters routed out of cypress boards for the parks: "We Prohibit . . . , No . . . , No . . . , and No . . ." Spiky green on white for zoos: "Do Not . . . , . . . Not Allowed, . . . Is Prohibited." *And-we-mean-it* black and white for commercial establishments: "Absolutely NO . . . , . . . Are Required, We Forbid . . ."

I imagine, one night, as he works late stacking and bundling signs for the next day's delivery, the tendril of a grapevine creeps in at his window. When his back is turned, its pale nose will gently nudge itself around him.

"No Touching!" he will admonish.

But with a clutch and a snatch the vine will retract, and he will find himself yanked through the night sky above a central Florida state park.

"Do Not Swing from Vines!" he will shriek.

And with that, the vine will untwine and drop him into the vortex of a limpid spring.

"No Swimming!" he will sputter as the dark, icy water closes over his head. As he sinks, strange, pale-colored fish will swim up and cock their eyes at him. "Do Not Feed the Fish," he will squeak. But, slowly and precisely, the fish will angle up, move in, and then, all over, he will feel the pick pick pick of those prickly lips.

Hot Springs

Hot springs: there's good ones and bad ones.
The worst hot springs are the ones behind
chain-link fences in shabby little western
towns where the sulphurous water is piped
into blue concrete pools that are filled from
May through October with fat, sluggish people in bathing suits who spread themselves
around on the underwater ledges and yell
at their children in the adjoining municipal
pool. Hairs float by, caught up in bits of
scum; close to the surface of the water a
faint smell of urine transcends the sulphur;
and on the sidewalks permanent pools of
warm, stagnant water swelter and fester,
spawning Blis-To-Sol–resistant strains of
athlete's foot.

Not much better are the trendy "healing"
springs near fashionable Far West urban cen-
ters, with Spanish tile pathways lined with
terra-cotta pots of red geraniums and blue

stokesia, establishments offering special features like herbal sweat wraps, salt scrubs, and rejuvenating facial masks made of green mud discovered by Indians. Wan-looking women whose pale linen and silk sheaths match their hair color wander around in a trancelike state, and everywhere is the scent of damp humans and sage. The hot tiles burn your feet as you make your way from the lithium pool to the iron pool, and in the last and hottest pool, containing traces of arsenic, a woman draped in healing crystals and submerged to the chin describes to another bather the macrobiotic diet she is following to cure her systemic bacterial infection.

I don't really like getting into small pools of hot water with so many other people, who, after all, are probably there because of some health or hygiene disorder. Scrofulous ulcers spring to mind. After a few tense minutes of submersion, feeling my skin prickle with permeability, I just have to give up the healing waters, rinse off in the shower, where the water is cool and smells comfortingly of chlorine, dry myself with my own towel, giving special attention between the toes, and drive back out into the desert.

There is a hot spring in the mountains of western Virginia where I do feel safe, though, and if not healed, at least soothed and comforted. The best time to go there is in April, when the grass is new and green, the ground is still spongy from melted snow, some trees don't yet have their leaves but the lilacs are coming into bloom, and the sunlight has a sprightly brightness. The hot baths (gentlemen and ladies bathe separately) are enclosed in gracious old Victorian buildings covered in hundreds of layers of white paint. There is a little lattice gazebo where you can dip up a drink of hot mineral water from a covered well in the floor. The ladies' bathhouse is round, with little chinks of windows. The tall conical roof is open at the top, so that a circle of sunlight shines down into the pool.

Silent bathers drift in and out of that wobbly circle of light, submerged to their ears, their eyes closed, their arms and legs gently flapping. Some of them wear cotton bathing garments, different shades of brown with enormous russet and mauve flowers or stripes, which billow out to the sides like the wings of a tropical ray, and some of them are naked. In the light that streams down through the hole in the roof they look pale and almost translucent, like giant jellyfish.

The water is clear, and the floor of the pool is lined with smooth round stones. Floating in that hot water with the high disk of cold blue sky above and the warm brown stones below, I can feel the thoughts leaving my head. The little ones go first: squeak in brakes, are my feet becoming larger, forgot to check box Do Not Send This Month's Selection. Then ideas begin seeping out: time and aging, perception of beauty in nature connected with personal involvement, why dead people don't contact me. At last a random slurry of images floats up and drifts away — Anasazi Indian petroglyph, two swans in Suffolk County, Thomas Alva Edison asleep under a laboratory table — until finally my mind is like an empty white room, the bare floor swept clean, the tall windows stripped of curtains.

I float and float, wandering around in the light and air of that room, enjoying myself, until at last I pause to look out one of those tall windows, and see that it is spring in western Virginia, and the lilacs are in bloom.

Saltville

I stopped at the scenic overlook, just to get a good deep breath before I went down into town. I was going to Saltville, Virginia, to help my great-aunt Della move out of her rickety old two-story house and into an old folks' home in Roanoke, where everything is on one level, and where by day she can sit on plastic-covered sofas with people her own age, and by night she can lie between clean sheets breathing the smell of antiseptics and listening to the death rattle of the window air conditioner in her own room.

I looked down on the houses lining the steep streets of Saltville. Some of them are new brick houses, but most of them are like my aunt's, tall and narrow with double windows in the gable. In the middle of town is the Saltine Motel. A couple of white vans from the university were parked at the motel's restaurant, and on the west edge of town the paleontologists were at work. Even from this far away I could see them toiling over their numbered squares of mud. They had reached the water table this year, and I could barely hear the hum of the pumps draining off the water that seeps into the pit.

On the east of town is the cemetery on its knoll. Some of General J. E. B. Stuart's family are buried near the entrance.

Beyond the cemetery is the old saltworks, which supplied most of the salt for the Confederacy during the Civil War. It is the site of one of the worst atrocities of the war, the Saltville Massacre, during which hundreds of wounded black soldiers fighting for the Union were murdered after the Battle of Saltville in 1864.

What with the paleontologists digging the agatized bones of prehistoric animals out of the mud on one end of town, the historians poking around the saltworks on the other, and General Stuart's loved ones buried in full view of the scene of the massacre, Saltville is not a very peaceful place to be dead in, I thought. Then I took my deep breath and went down.

My aunt greeted me at the street, and we walked slowly between her borders of Shasta daisies and phlox to the porch. I helped her over the rough spots where the bricks have humped up, and we carefully skirted the rotten boards in the porch floor. She brought us lemonade in glasses that were not exactly clean, and we sat in her cluttered living room and talked.

"Really, Aunt Della, with Uncle Henry dead and Alice gone, what have you got to keep you in Saltville besides the cats and the flowers?"

"My life," she said.

But we both knew she couldn't stay in that house. The roof leaked, and the front porch was falling off. In Roanoke she would be safe. We agreed to start clearing out in the morning.

I slept upstairs in the front room with the double windows. It was a hot, still night, and I left the windows open. The dingy lace curtains drooped limply, there was a smell of mildew, and I could hear the hum of the water pumps at the dig site all night long.

I had made up my mind at the Scenic Overlook to make a clean sweep through the house. I would not allow myself to be distracted by emotional things. The books would go to the Saltville Library, the clothes to the Goodwill, and the furniture would be sold at auction. But when I opened the tall leaded glass doors to the bookcase and that cool winey-scented air fell down on me, I lost my resolve. There were all the books I had read during my childhood summers in Saltville.

Aunt Della stoically dragged up an empty box. "Start with Dickens," she said stoutly.

But I was looking at the Palliser novels. "Nobody reads Trollope anymore," I mused.

"And yet," said Aunt Della, taking down *The Duke's Children*, "I've always been in love with Phineas Finn."

I hadn't even started yet, but I had to take a break. Aunt Della and I went down to the Saltine Motel Restaurant. We sat in the air-conditioning and listened to a waitress trying to explain the menu to a historian from the University of Virginia.

"Just because you see it on the menu, that doesn't mean we have it. It just means we might have it. If it's not on the menu, that means we never have it."

I noticed that the historian kept watching us, and after a while he got up and made his way to our table.

Aunt Della introduced me to him. "You were given your great-great-grandfather's name," Mr. Colson said to me. He sat down across from Aunt Della and leaned toward her attentively. "Are you ready to talk to me, Mrs. Meadows?" he asked.

Aunt Della gave me a furtive glance. "Yes,"

she said, "tonight. Come at six o'clock."

We headed back to the house. I had hoped that the cool impersonal air in the Saltine Motel Restaurant would bring me to my senses. I held my breath and opened the bookcase doors. I quickly packed up Dickens and started on Trollope. But when I came to *Phineas Finn* I had to stop. I went out and sat on the porch with Aunt Della. "What was that all about? What about six o'clock?" I asked.

"You know," she said, "your great-great-grandfather was on General Stuart's staff during the war. Then he was on General Lee's staff. He was an engineer with the Army of Northern Virginia. And he was with Jackson at the Battle of Malvern Hill. Mr. Colson is a student of history, and he is interested in these things."

I took a walk in the late afternoon. I walked to the cemetery and leaned up against the gravestone of a nephew of General Stuart. I read four chapters of *Phineas Finn*. After all, I told myself, I have a whole week. It will be easier tomorrow.

When I got back to the house, Mr. Colson was sitting at the kitchen table. Aunt Della had laid a tea towel in front of him, and from a box she took out a letter and smoothed it open.

"You should see this," she said to me. "It's a letter from Mrs. Lee to your great-great-grandfather Bailey."

The letter was dated November 1870. The handwriting was neat and prim. I could read parts of it over Mr. Colson's shoulder:

> I feel most tender interest in all who served . . . gratification to know how they honor him . . . every duty faithfully performed . . . never spared himself or looked for reward . . . with pleasure for your memorial work . . . a lock of General Lee's hair, for which as you suppose I have had many applications.

Then Aunt Della took a folded yellow card out of the box. She laid it in front of Mr. Colson and opened it. Inside was a curved lock of steel-gray hair secured with a straight pin.

Mr. Colson stood up. He held his hands behind his back and said, "Mrs. Meadows, for your grandfather's personal handwritten account of his experiences of the war, for the letter to him from J. E. B. Stuart, for the letter from Mary Custis Lee with the photographs of herself and General Lee, and the lock of General Lee's hair I will pay you fifty thousand dollars."

Today, a year later, I stop again at the Scenic Overlook. There's progress in Saltville, Aunt Della told me on the phone. The paleontologists have found a bear's tooth — the earliest evidence of carnivores at this dig site. And the historians have uncovered evidence that the Saltville Massacre may have been perpetrated by deserters and marauders, so no general or men under his command should carry the blame. The Saltine Motel Restaurant has adjusted to the increase in trade and is doing a booming business.

The porch no longer sags on Aunt Della's house. There's a shiny new sheet-metal roof, and the bleached lace curtains float in the windows. Trollope and Dickens are in their places on the bookshelves, the floors gleam, and the house smells sweetly of Murphy's Oil Soap.

At the cemetery the big poplar trees shade the graves of the Stuarts, and Queen Anne's lace and pink clover are blooming all over the hill. As I fall asleep in the upstairs room with the two windows open, I listen to the humming of the pumps and think what good use the people of Saltville make of their dead.

One-Room Schoolhouse

I am always saddened, driving through small towns in the United States, to come upon the old schoolhouse. Sometimes it is a grand brick building with ivy and an avenue of oak trees leading up to its high granite steps and arched doorway. Sometimes it is a stone schoolhouse with tall windows. In little villages it is often a white clapboard building with a hip roof and a bell tower. But one thing you can be almost sure of: it won't be a school anymore.

If the town is sad and poor, the old schoolhouse will be abandoned, with broken windows, rotting door frames, and graffiti spray-painted on its walls. If the town is lucky and imaginative, the old schoolhouse will have been transformed into offices and condominiums, or little craft shops reeking of potpourri made from wood shavings soaked in synthetic oil of cinnamon.

In Granville, Vermont (population 309), the old schoolhouse is downtown, next to the town hall. It's a white clapboard building with green trim and a steep roof. In the high front gable a plaque says 1857. The paint is bright, the picket fence in the front is in good shape. And on a spring day in 1991 when I pushed open the schoolhouse's heavy paneled door and stepped inside, there were no weary office workers in their cubicles separated by imitation wood-grain partition walls, or chatty tourists buying Kountry Krafts and miniature plastic jugs of maple syrup. Instead, in this old one-room school-house there were actually students — seventeen little girls and boys aged six through eleven, and their teacher, Ms. Roland. They were all attentively going about the business of reading and writing and doing arithmetic, just as many of their parents and grandparents and great-grandparents had done at Granville School since 1857.

Of course, changes have been made. Under the five east windows that look out across the snowy playground to the great red barn of the farm next door, four computers sat on a shelf, and under one of the high windows at the back of the schoolroom a reading loft had been constructed. There was a copy machine and a TV set, and two bathrooms in the back.

Still, in Vermont some things never change. On one computer Nathan was writing to his pen pal in Maine:

Dear Tina,
I'm fine. I've been maple sugaring. Do you sugar?

From Nathan

At a desk seven-year-old Amanda sat in a bright stream of early spring sunlight working her way through a sheet full of addition and subtraction problems with numbers in the hundreds. She carried and borrowed, and crossed out digits and changed tens into ones and counted on her fingers. Gabe was writing quite cleverly about ice fishing, "It's fun, but it's cool," and Preston was making several very intricate paper airplanes with down-turned wingtips and angled noses, but he knew better than to fly them in the classroom.

In the tiny school kitchen, Mr. Bannister, the cook at Granville School, was making lunch. He stirred the gravy and looked out the south-facing windows at the bleak little town. "This is mud season," he told me apologetically. "But in the fall it's like a quilt with all the colors."

After lunch (turkey and rice, beans, bread,

and birthday cake) the children bundled into their tired winter clothes and filed outside to romp around in the mud. Ms. Roland and I stood on a stomped-down patch of snow talking about the fate of schoolhouses and the joys and drudgeries of schoolteaching. A little girl came up and leaned against Ms. Roland, her damp mittens dangling from the insides of her stained coat sleeves. We gazed at a mountain in the distance, all gray and black and white.

"Ms. Roland," the little girl asked wistfully, "what is spring?"

Then it was quiet-time at Granville School. Justin sat in a chair at the front of the class and read aloud from *Bears on Hemlock Mountain*. Preston made another airplane and a pretty little folded paper box. Faye colored a butterfly. Ginger made a cover out of a cereal box for a book she had written about her twenty-five-year-old horse, Beaver (he eats trees), and several children glued little outfits on rabbits they had cut out of poster board. There were the eternal school smells of chalk dust, wax crayons, cedar shavings, damp wool, and warm children.

I looked out the window and thought about Granville's struggles to keep its one-room school. In 1989 the town had voted down a petition to close the school and bus the seventeen Granville students to Rochester Elementary. Then the Americans with Disabilities Act decreed that if Granville could not provide its students with a handicapped toilet, the school would have to be shut down. But out the window, gleaming in the unfiltered sunlight, I could see the brand-new maze of covered walkways and angled ramps Granville citizens had erected to connect the town hall, the town clerk's office, and the school to the one wheelchair-accessible toilet in town.

The people in Granville don't seem to care that the handicapped toilet is now the hub of their downtown. They just know that while other children are getting their educations in squat, energy-efficient, modern school buildings made all of concrete and plastic, with squinny-eyed chinks of windows, here in Granville, for one more year at least, a little girl, wondering about spring, can curl up on a pillow in the reading loft at quiet-time, and gaze through the ripply old glass at the woods behind the school where, quite soon now, the buds on the trees will begin to swell.

Fish Camp

There's a smell of stagnant water and roses and cigarette smoke in the open air. There's the gurgling hum of the circulating pump and the flash of wild shiners in the concrete bait tanks. Occasionally the high-pitched *"eeee"* of an eagle can be heard overhead, and at night there are the thumps of armadillos under the floors of the shabby little cabins, and from the creek and swamp the raucous squawk of limpkins.

In the screened front room of the main building there are a Coke machine, a cricket box, and a display of garishly colored rubber worms, and under a scratched-up pane of glass on the counter are photographs of filthy, happy people, mostly barefoot, holding the fish they have caught — warmouth perch, bluegills and shellcrackers, sunshine bass, largemouth bass, speckled perch, crappie. Below each picture, important information is printed carefully with a permanent marker:

SWEET TALKER BUZZ BAIT
OCTOBER 27, 1987 — 7½ POUNDS

I came down here to central Florida with my brother, who likes to fish. But on this afternoon I stay on the porch with Annie, and we watch my brother's little boat skim down the canal and out into the black water of Lake Lochloosa.

"Georgia," says Annie. "That's nothing new. They come from all over — Connecticut, Kentucky, Tennessee, Michigan, Alabama, Louisiana, Illinois, Wisconsin. They come to fish, honey, and they keep on coming back every year, until they pass away."

Annie is a big woman. She has a slow and thorough way of moving, like an old elephant who knows his business. Annie has been owner and operator of Twin Lakes Fish Camp since 1974, through the bad years when the water was low and boats couldn't get in and out of the slips, through the sad years after her first husband dropped down dead of a heart attack on a fishing expedition, and into this year — a good wet spring, plenty of water in the lakes and the creek, the wild roses in full bloom along the canal, and Ted, an industrious cousin retired from the military, repairing boat motors on weekends.

Annie takes a contemplative drag on her cigarette. "Oh yes," she says, "they're old when they come. Only trouble is, they get to be like family, you see, and it tears you up when they pass away."

Inside, the house is dark and cool. On the walls are framed prints of herons and egrets in cypress swamps and watery glades. But the pictures look dry and dull compared to the view out any of Annie's windows, where every green thing glistens, the water in the lakes and creek glows black, and even the air shimmers with light and moisture.

On the kitchen table are strewn the body parts of a dismantled wooden Easter bunny. Annie carefully puts him together — his pair of pink-lined ears, back legs, and tail fit into sawed-out slots on his back — and sets him up on the Formica tabletop. She stands back and gives him a look.

"Harry made him," she says. "Harry's one of my boyfriends. That's why I got so many china cabinets, honey, to put all this stuff they give me." Sure enough, the walls are lined with glass-fronted cabinets, and every shelf is filled with objects of art and craft, neatly arranged.

"Yep," says Annie, "Harry, he misdialed

the telephone one day up in Gainesville, drunk, got me by mistake, came out to fish, and been coming ever since. Nine, ten years, out of Michigan."

Annie peers down into the bait tank, scoops out a dead shiner, and flips it over into a potted tomato plant.

"Most of them are nice," she says, "but you do get your funny ones, weird — well, different. I shouldn't say 'weird.' In the spring of the year, honey, most of them come out of Ohio."

Twin Lakes Fish Camp provides trailer hookups, tent camping sites, and several little cottages. In an effort to encourage good housekeeping Annie has put up neatly lettered signs in the kitchens:

DO NOT CLEAN FISH IN THE SINK
PLEASE WASH UP

The cottages are neat and clean, with stacks of mismatched towels and washrags in the bathrooms, plastic dishes in the kitchen cupboards, and an assortment of fish-cleaning gadgets in the drawers. But the floors feel spongy with moisture, and the air is saturated with the smell of mildew and fried fish. Behind the cabins are a bait house and a vegetable garden, and across the path are the boat slip, with boats and canoes lined up under a tin-roofed shed, and a ramp where you can launch your own boat (one dollar).

"There goes Sam Martin," says Annie. A spidery looking old man climbs carefully down into a boat and gently nudges it out into the slip. "He's an old bachelor, never been married. All he's got is high blood pressure. He's been coming since 1978, and still fishing. Now there's some of them don't fish. Thelma, she don't fish. She just comes down and stays in a travel trailer six months. Thelma's from New Hampshire. She's into the peace movement, picketing, all that. Went to Mississippi to help them two gay-lesbian women. Been coming down here six years."

Annie is the only woman fish camp owner in Alachua County. "They wanted to see me go under," she says. "They wanted to see me fall on my face. I had to outlast 'em. Now I'm the only one still here — but one, Jimmy Easterbrook at North Bank Fish Camp. We're buddies now. I told him, 'Jimmy, if you give up, I'll give up.' See, honey, I'm one of them determinationed people."

Annie hauls herself out of her chair, nets a shiner from the tank, and throws it out the screen door. A big white heron gallops out of the creek on his gawky orange legs and gobbles it up. Then he saunters delicately back down the bank where he poses gracefully, surrounded by shining black and green.

"That's Fred," says Annie. She continues, "Yep, in '89 the water was so low there was grass growing in the boat slip. Had to mow it with a lawn mower. Weeds higher than your head in the canal — we cut 'em with a Weed Eater. Three years of drought. I had ulcers from the stress, honey. I was afraid to lose everything. But one Sunday in 1991 I went to church and I told Him, 'I can't do nothing about this, Lord, it's your problem. I'm trucking on with my life.' And I did."

Annie takes me on a tour of the fish camp. She shows me the fishy-smelling bait house, with tanks of wild shiners, grass shrimp, and minnows. She shows me the little pepper, cucumber, and tomato plants she has started in plastic tubs, the boat slip, and the "couples cabin." It has a basket filled with old *Woman's Day* magazines, ruffled curtains at the windows, and framed pictures of kittens and fawns on the walls. She shows me the metal shed up the hill where she gives parties.

"My birthday one year they brought me two bushels of oysters. We ate oysters every which way — raw, fried, stewed, and steamed. And, honey, Thanksgiving and

Christmas?" She lays a hand on my arm and says confidentially, "I've got people, before they pass away, rather have Thanksgiving and Christmas with me than home with the kids."

She shows me a giant turnip plant someone gave her. "It's my monster," she says, and it is taller than she is, with thick deep green leaves. She digs up a runner for me from another plant with flowers that look like red pinecones, and wraps it up in wet newspaper.

"Dan Ross, why he's alive I don't know," Annie says. "Five bypasses. Doctors in Fargo, North Dakota, told him to go home and die. He turned around and drove down here, walked into the clinic in McIntosh having a heart attack. Told me if he died, have him cremated. They told him, 'She can't do that, she don't have power of attorney.' Dan's a sweetheart. He don't fish, now, on account of his health."

We settle back down on Annie's screen porch. The sun is lower now, and the sounds have changed from the bright midday chirps and whistles to the settling-in sounds of late afternoon. Annie's cousin Ted and his wife come up on the porch, and Harry comes in from cleaning fish. He's wearing short pants and flip-flops. Annie gives him a hug and takes him in to show him how cute his Easter bunny looks all put together on the kitchen table. Then they all sit in the plastic sofas and chairs on the porch and smoke cigarettes and talk about fishing. Annie says she and Dan Ross are going to go marlin fishing. Ted tells her she'll get seasick. Harry tells her you have to pull four, five hours to land a marlin.

We look out at the canal, and they tell me about the developer who was inspired by the movie version of *Cross Creek* to turn one of the uninhabited islands in Lake Lochloosa into a town with stores, houses, and a golf course. Local residents put a stop to it, and ospreys and bald eagles continue to build their nests in the giant old cypress trees and long-leafed pines on the island.

"There's one eagle around here runs with a buzzard," says Annie. "They fly around, eat roadkill together. I says to myself, Now that's different."

There is still light in the sky, but the sun has disappeared behind the trees when my brother comes in. While he hauls up his boat, Annie gets her clippers. I stand around and slap mosquitoes in her backyard while she picks me an armload of Don Juan roses to take home.

"Listen, honey," she says to me, "don't pay any attention to them. I've got my plans:

there's one thing me and Dan Ross are going to do before he passes away, and that's go marlin fishing."

Annie stands in the road and waves goodbye to my brother and me. Then she turns and with that steady and ponderous gait she heads back up to the porch.

Something Old, Something New

I went to a wedding in south Florida. It took place in a tenth-century Spanish monastery that had been packaged up and shipped to the United States in the 1920s. Then, because of some shift in William Randolph Hearst's whimsy, and the threat of hoof-and-mouth disease, the old stones ended up sitting in a warehouse in Brooklyn, New York, in eleven thousand wooden crates for fifty years until they were bought by a south Florida Christian philanthropist and reassembled in north Miami.

We strolled through the courtyard, landscaped with the monster houseplants of south Florida, and were seated by rank in the nave of the old church. We waited in our fine clothes listening to "Prelude in C Minor" and breathed the cool, damp air seeping out of the stone walls. When we heard the wedding march begin, we all rose in unison and turned with our bright, expectant smiles. But instead of the radiant bride sweeping to the altar on her father's arm, here came, marching backward and clothed all in black like Japanese puppeteers, the photographer and his assistant. He had shoulder-length, gleaming black ringlets of hair, a pointy beard, and wore a tailcoat. She was dressed in black gauze and held a strobe light aloft like a mitre.

After that moment of horror we recovered ourselves, and sure enough, here came the bride. She is a statuesque, capable woman, who has an interest in deep-sea diving and is said to be able to free dive to fifty-one feet. In the glare of the photographer's lights her great gleaming shoulders and chest seemed to rise out of the white froth of her wedding dress like Venus from the foam.

Except for the priest hired for this occasion missing the groom's middle name by one consonant, the ceremony came off without a hitch, and soon we were back in the courtyard drinking clear iced drinks with tiny straws.

A lost family friend I hadn't seen in years suddenly began telling me that her husband's diaries and daily logs from his tour of duty in Vietnam had been stolen, along with all his power tools.

"He won't talk about those years," she said. "Those records were all he had." We sipped our drinks, and she told me that she has begun taking in stray animals — six cats so far, and a blind rottweiler. "If he would just talk about it," she said. "He's never told me about it in all these years."

Through the fleshy limbs and glabrous leaves of a giant jade tree I could see my niece Lucy, dressed in shimmering green, talking to a couple of tiny little aunts of ours — old native Floridians who remembered when downtown Fort Lauderdale was a tomato farm, and who had the idea that they had formed the whole state of Florida with their own white-gloved hands and were now having it wrested away by a generation of ruffians who had never learned the basic rules of etiquette. I could tell by the stricken look on Lucy's face that they were telling her yet again how she could be a much better person if she would change her whole life, and how she too might soon be a bride, if only . . .

Most of the men in my family are color-blind, but something about the angle of the setting sun and the miracle fiber in Lucy's dress made them suddenly able to see the color green for the first time. So before I could rescue Lucy from the aunts, my brother and several nephews and cousins had shoved them away and were gathered around Lucy stroking her dress and murmuring reverently, "Green, that's green!"

After the sun went down, the dancing began. First the bride danced with her father, and the groom danced with his mother, but that was the last dancing that was done by any rules. Lucy, her green dress shimmering in the moonlight like the glistening skin of a tropical frog, danced with the woman whose husband had lost his Vietnam records. The bride, rising higher and higher out of her wedding dress as the night went on, danced all by herself. Around the edge, under the roof of the old monastery, the tiny little aunts sat in their pastel dresses with their tight lips, and in the alcoves and vaulted niches, my brother with his magnifying glass to his eye dated the stones by examining the fossilized remains of the prehistoric creatures preserved in them and murmured the names of aeons under his breath.

Cumberland Island

Every year, in the bleak dawn of midwinter, my oldest friend and I drive across the state of Georgia to the coast, where we get on a ferryboat and ride to Cumberland Island. Some years the weather is bright and everything sparkles, but I prefer it the way it is this year — a gray, lowering sky and a mist that might turn into rain.

Most of the island is covered by a maritime forest of live oak trees with a dense understory of palmettos. The trees form a canopy over the white sandy trail that runs the length of the island, so that you can't see the sky, only the twisting, arching limbs of the great trees overhead. On this drizzly winter day, the colors up close seem dense, so that the bright green of the palmettos looks almost greasy; while in the distance everything is cloaked in the gray mist.

After two or three miles of walking down

that road we see, rising out of the wilderness, an old wrought-iron gate, fancifully ornamented with scrolls and flourishes. We go through that gate out of the forest gloom and into the winter afternoon light of the grounds of Dungeness. In the middle of the ragged lawn it still stands, or what's left of it still stands — the ruins of the castle against the gray clouds. Through the tall paired windows of the remaining walls of the upper stories you can see the sky, and from a lower window a scruffy wild pony looks out at us. On one edge of the lawn, curving steps lead down into what must have once been a water garden with lily ponds and shaded walks. Now the steps end in a kind of stagnant slough. Grapevines swag down from overhead, and tree roots are crumbling the bricks.

The little pony follows us for a while as we walk to the old inn where we will spend the night. It's too cold to sit on the wide front porch, so all the guests are sunk into the down cushions on the sofas and rocking chairs in the big front room. The only sounds are the ticking of the clock on the stairway, the crunch of a log crumbling in the fireplace, and the footsteps of an ancient tailless cat walking across the rug.

My friend and I want to talk, so we creep

down to the deserted library at the other end of the hall. In this room the windows face north. The furniture is dark, a squat table lamp spreads out a meager circle of light, and the floor-to-ceiling shelves display a collection of the world's dullest books. We stretch out our tired legs and drink cups of tea we have brought up from the pantry. We talk about all the same things we've talked about for the past twenty-five years.

At dusk we put on our coats again and go out. Of course, we can't see the sunset, shrouded as we are by forest, but we watch the night come. It seems to soak down through the trees. Looking in the dining-room windows we can see the gleaming tablecloth and the white plates with their little pink rose borders being laid for our supper. There's a smell of garlic and baking bread.

That night as I lie under a blanket and quilt in my cold little white upstairs bedroom I imagine that I can hear the sound of the ocean seeping through the walls.

The morning of our last day on the island is brighter. We walk purposefully down the road this time, because we want to get to the old Stafford place by noon, and it's a long way. After a few miles we come out of the virgin oak forests and into abandoned fields and second-growth woods of slash pine. Now we are in the part of Cumberland Island that was cleared for the cultivation of cotton, rice, and indigo in the early 1800s. Within an old tabby wall are the grounds of the Stafford house, burned down over a hundred years ago. The road we're walking on, shaded by ancient cedar and magnolia trees, is the same road the plantation people used, and the Indians before them.

Before long we come to a clearing where fourteen or fifteen chimneys still stand, all that remain of the Stafford slave quarters. They stand in a straight row, neat and orderly, facing south. Each one has its silvery gray live-oak lintel, still supporting the column of lovely pink brick. Halfway down the row of chimneys is the well. We look down into it, through the fern fronds that have sprouted on the slimy sides of the brick walls, and see the circle of black water, with the ferns, our faces, and the sky reflected in it. We think about all we've learned about this place, and all we will never know.

On our walk back to the ferry dock that afternoon we make one last detour to the beach. We stand on a high sand dune and look out at the sea and the imposing gray sky. On the horizon, I see something black heave up, curve over, and then a spray of white water shoots up into the sky. I squint and stare. I see it again. I grab my friend's arm and point. "Whales!" I say. We lean forward and stare into the gray. Again and again we see the black curve and the white spray.

"It's just waves breaking," my friend says. And we turn back into the comforting gloom of the forest and walk down the last stretch of white sandy road.

"Whales!" My friend laughs at me. I feel a little embarrassed. I don't mention the whales again.

But driving home that evening in the holiday traffic of Interstate 10, through the bitter winter rain that has finally resolved itself from the gentle mists of Cumberland Island, I wonder, Why couldn't they have been whales, after all the wonderful things we have seen and felt these past two days? And, anyway, why would waves be breaking so far out at sea?

Nursery

My neighbor Luther and I were driving through a light rain over to a fruit tree nursery in south Alabama. We had a list: a satsuma, two kumquat trees, a lime, and three mulberries. Luther was worrying that the fruit tree man would get too close to him. Luther is squeamish.

"The man never bathes," he said.

"But he knows his fruit trees," I said. That is why we keep going back to the fruit tree man, in spite of Luther's persnickety ways. The fruit tree man works his orchard like an Oriental martial art. He maintains an exquisite balance of nutrients with organic fertilizers he mixes himself. He prunes with such care that his trees and their root systems complement each other perfectly, and every fruit is born within arm's reach. And he performs magical feats of grafting, so that one single citrus tree will bear limes, lemons, grapefruits, and oranges.

The fruit tree man came bustling out and met us at the gate. First there is his nose, big and strange and covered with odd swellings. It looks as if it had been formed from the mass of five normal noses, melted down, and then shaped into this one nose before it was quite cool enough to handle. Then the eyes: one eye looks you in the face earnestly; while the other eye goes skittering off and then fixes its lizardlike gaze on something over your right shoulder. The hands are big and red and rough, and both thumbnails have been deformed by gardening into little black horns, like the dewclaws on a dog.

"Hey man," the fruit tree man said. "Hey man, what's up, man?"

Luther is not exactly a "Hey man" sort of fellow. He took a step back and held his arms close to his sides.

"Man," said the fruit tree man, "have I got one far-out tree to show you." He cocked his eyebrow and fixed Luther with his one good eye. "Oriental, man."

Luther fumbled in his pocket for the list. "A Satsuma, two kumquats, a lime, and . . . ," he said, but he was too slow.

The fruit tree man grabbed us and hauled us through a jungle of fruit trees. On the limes and lemons great wads of blooms up and down the branches swarmed with bees, and the limbs of the persimmon trees drooped and swagged under the weight of the great golden fruits. There was the smell of fermenting figs and citrus blossoms and ginger lilies and bonemeal and sulphur-coated urea. The fruit tree man was wearing filthy dirty trousers held together across the thighs by a few ragged warp threads, enormous old wallowed out sneakers with no socks, no shirt, and around his neck a shred of the blue bandana he wore on a hitchhiking trip out west in 1968 when he walked down into the Grand Canyon and ate peyote.

The fruit tree man is an old hippie. As lost as he's been all these years among his fruit trees in the wilds of south Alabama, the 1980s and 1990s have passed him by without a trace.

"Some nights, man, you want to get a little high, take a little toke, do a little weed?" The fruit tree man rubbed his horny thumbs against his forefingers then poked Luther in the chest. "Man, I got the tree for you." And we stopped in front of a little droopy tree, maybe five feet high, covered with oval red fruits. The fruit tree man raised both hands, palms up, to the little tree: "Jujube!"

I picked one of the little red fruits and

bit into it. The skin snapped. The flavor was like a mild pear.

The fruit tree man stood back and looked at me. "Just wait," he said. "You'll feel a warm glow, starting at your feet. Then you'll feel like this great calmness. Hey man," he said to Luther, "Oriental women, they eat this fruit when they go into labor. They get so blissed out they don't feel the pain."

We bought our trees: a satsuma, two kumquats, a lime, three mulberries — and one jujube. On the way home Luther started to fret about me. He was worried I'd become too calm to drive. He decided I should get something in my stomach, give the jujube time to wear off before we started the long drive home in the rain.

We went into a little concrete block restaurant in Bayline. Inside it was dark and still. It was an odd time of day for a meal, so Luther and I were the only diners. Dusty plastic plants hung from the low ceiling, and the walls were decorated with black-and-white photographs showing people and their fish. Out the south window by our table we saw a tattered palm tree, a scabby piece of lawn, a tiny beach, then the gulf, flat and smooth. A drizzly rain was falling. The water and the sky were the same shade of gray.

"I do feel calm," I told Luther. I ate crackers and drank tea and tried to figure out where the sky began. Suddenly the smooth water broke, and a porpoise arched out of it, a darker shade of gray.

The windows in the north wall looked out at the backyard of the restaurant. There were some boats turned upside down on the ground, then the palmetto and pinewoods of south Alabama. Out this window the sun was shining. The sky was bright blue, and the woods glowed with light. Everything glistened. I could hear birds singing. It was like watching two different days at the same time out the windows at the Bayline restaurant. Luther pushed the basket of crackers over to me. He looked worried.

"You look blissed out," he said. "Do you feel that you are about to give birth to an Oriental baby?"

I thought about the smooth patina of filth on the skin of the fruit tree man and his wandering eye fixed on something in another time. I remembered the little snap of the red skin on the jujube, and the smells of sulphur-coated urea, citrus blossoms, and rotting fruit. Then, all at once, out the windows on the bay side of the restaurant the clouds parted, rays of sunlight beamed down, the water changed from lead gray to a warm blue-green, the tiny white sandy beach sparkled, and the sunny day spread itself out over the Gulf of Mexico.

"Without so much as a whimper," I said.

Walking Horses

There's the smell of hay and cracked corn
and leather and molasses and saddle soap.
But mostly there's the sweetly rotten smell
of horses' feet, because horses' feet are the
most important thing on a Tennessee walking
horse farm. In one stall a big black stallion
ramps back and forth, looking out through
the chain-link window with his wild wide
eyes. His neck curls; his nostrils flare and
tremble. He gives a snort. Elmer claps him
on the shoulder. "Hyah deah! Hyah deah!"
he says. The horse gives another snort and
settles down. The horse's name is Magic,
and Elmer is his trainer.

Elmer is a solitary man. His wife left him
years ago to live with a motorcycle repairman
in Reno, and Elmer's son wandered off soon
after his sixteenth birthday and never came
back. Elmer doesn't have a home. He just
has a big pickup truck, a four-horse trailer,

an assortment of tack, and tools for working on horses' feet. He lives with the horses he trains.

Elmer doesn't talk much. A lifetime spent with walking horses has permanently impaired his speech. Now he speaks to people the same way he speaks to horses, with guttural, emphatic utterances that might once have been words. "Dah yu go! Dah yu go!" is an expression of approval and appreciation. "Wachess, wachess!" means "Be careful."

Elmer leads Magic out of the stall and stands him on a concrete pad. He ties him up to two posts with nylon straps fastened to each side of Magic's halter. He runs his hands down Magic's front legs, feeling for ominous warm spots and lumps. Then he picks up the stallion's feet one at a time. Magic's front feet are huge. He is wearing big stacked-up shoes with metal straps over the top of the hoof, fastened with a turn-buckle on the outside. The shoes are made of layers of rubber, with three wedge-shaped sections between the layers so that the horse's hooves tip forward slightly. Elmer fastens chains around Magic's fetlocks, just above the high feet. Then he puts on a bridle and saddle.

Elmer is fat. His big belly hangs out from under his short T-shirt. He hauls himself up onto Magic's back and arranges his belly with both hands over the saddle horn. He leans forward and says, "Geeyah!" With a gawky, clunky gait Magic lurches slowly across the yard. Elmer stops him at the road. He hauls him around with the reins to get him in position. There is some backing up, some awkward tangling of legs, then clumsy realignment. Magic chomps his bit. He stands still, his feet rooted to the ground, his knees locked. Then Elmer gathers up the reins, leans back, and pulls his legs back, toes down in the stirrups. Magic's head comes up. He tucks in his chin.

"Heejyah!" Elmer shouts, and Magic takes off. His glistening black mane flies, and with each step he lifts his knees up and up; then his feet lunge out, "break," and come down. The gait is called a "running walk," and the horse seems to fly down the road. Clods of dirt shoot out. Behind the flying mane Elmer sits, leaning back, absolutely still. His legs just hang there. His belly does not even jostle. Magic's high muscular shoulders thrust and pump and flex. His knees seem to pause at the top of each lift. It's called an "enhanced gait." But only the front part of the horse has been enhanced. It's as if there has been an enormous oversight on the part of the Tennessee Walking Horse Breeders and Exhibitors Association. For, from his powerful shoulders, chest, and magnificent front legs, Magic dwindles down toward his back end to a rather puny, plain-looking horse. His back legs are still the size of regular horse legs, and his back feet are just simple horse feet. They skitter along, in a hurry, struggling to keep up with the powerful front end. Fifty years of refining training techniques and equipment and breeding for selected deformities have created a monster out of a horse.

Elmer takes Magic up and down the road ten times. The reins scrape globs of froth off the stallion's neck and shoulders. Elmer's T-shirt is dark with sweat. Finally they stop. Magic's head comes down. He plants his front feet on the ground. His shoulders hunch forward. Behind him the road looks as if it has been harrowed. Elmer stands Magic on the concrete pad and rubs his legs. He tugs one leg up and examines the built-up shoe. Magic tosses his head. His muscles quiver. "Hyah deah! Hyah deah!" Elmer admonishes.

Someone brings out a tractor and pulls a roller up and down the road, smoothing it out. Elmer squirts Magic all over with a hose and scrapes the water off with a curved wand. He rubs liniment on the stallion's front legs and wraps them up in tape. Then, hobbling along on his chubby legs, his belly wagging with every step, he leads Magic to his stall. The horse follows obediently with his careful, lurching gait, his feet swinging out under the momentum of the ten-pound shoes. Elmer throws him a hand of hay and pours a scoop of sweet feed into his trough. There's the sound of horse lips swishing in the feed, then the peaceful *munch munch munch,* and Elmer's soothing murmur, "Dah yu go, dah yu go."

Large and Deep

I have the good fortune to live within an hour's drive of the world's largest and deepest spring. Four hundred thousand gallons of water a minute pour out of it, and intrepid divers have gone down far enough to discover a mastodon skeleton, and a race of pale blind shrimp, and water-filled caverns with vaulted ceilings three stories high. But no one has ever found the actual end, or beginning, of the spring.

Up the hill there's an old hotel with lovely sloping lawns and plantings of bridal-wreath spiraea, azaleas, camellias, and roses. Looking across the lawn from the porch of the hotel you can see the spring and its river, bordered with ancient cypress trees and water meadows of pickerelweed. You can change into your bathing suit in a bathhouse near the edge of the spring, and then with your face mask and snorkel pad along a mossy brick walkway down to the water's edge.

The water is crystal clear, and you float first over sparkling white sand; then the waving dark green blades of eelgrass brush your face; and then — and no matter how many times it happens you can't be ready for it — you float out over the head of the spring, and there's nothing below you but blackness. It makes you want to climb the air up into the blue sky. You gasp and whimper, then you float, staring into the dark, the faintest surge of water pressing up from below. At last you turn and paddle back over the eelgrass, then the sparkling white sand, and you climb out, a better and wiser person.

For some reason, people love to get married at this spring. There's always seemed to me to be a little touch of hubris in staging a wedding party in the presence of something so large and deep. But the graceful old hotel with its rose beds and its avenues of abelia, and the cool breeze from the spring, and the greenness of it all bring out the hymeneal tendencies in young people, so there is always a wedding or two in progress at the spring.

Last week it was a young cousin of mine and his bride. They had planned to have the ceremony in the wicker and lattice gazebo, with us wedding guests standing on the lawn in our pastel-colored clothes, wincing as they recited the wedding vows they had made up themselves. But a steady sprinkle of rain began to fall, the arching branches of the bridal-wreath spiraea began to droop and drip, and the whole thing had to be moved inside. The couple ended up exchanging their vows in the lobby of the hotel, between the mastodon tooth on its carved pedestal and the ten-foot-long stuffed alligator in his glass case.

Afterward we all went out on the porch and stood around in tight little groups, the groom's family and the bride's family eyeing each other suspiciously over limp cucumber sandwiches. The bridal couple, so sweet and so young, drank their glass of champagne and ate their piece of cake, then drove off with a flutter of pale blue and white satin. The wedding guests dispersed to their cars and drove home with their windshield wipers going *whoosh whoosh.*

For just a minute I stood on the flagstone floor of the porch and looked through the rain down over the lawns, now oozing green, to the spring. He would have done better, I thought, that young cousin of mine, to throw off his clothes and plunge into that water, to glide over the white sand and the dark waving blades of eelgrass, to the head of the spring, where he would slowly twirl and soar, looking down with his eyes wide open at so much blackness.

Produce Stand

FOR DUST THOU ART
AND UNTO DUST SHALT THOU RETURN
plums   peaches   watermelons

That's the message I read on the flashing
arrow sign as I drive by Mr. Grange's roadside
fruit and vegetable stand today. It's summer.
Cantaloupes and Persian melons are piled
up high in the bins, and ripening peaches
are spread out on the shelves. There's a
smell of mangoes and greengage plums, and
everywhere there are the colors of rose and
green and gold.

Mr. Grange is religious. His serious dark
eyes peering out of the shadow under the
brim of his Snap-On Tools cap look like
Noah's eyes must have looked when he
searched the horizon for that first sight of
land. Mr. Grange is looking for someone
from Idaho. On the back wall of the produce

shed hangs a schoolroom map of the continental United States. Every time new customers come in, Mr. Grange finds out where they are from. Then he sticks a tack in the map in that state. Tacks cover the states of Georgia, Alabama, South Carolina, and Florida like the scales on a reptile. There are two tacks in the state of Maine, four in California. But so far there is not a single tack in the state of Idaho.

Mr. Grange lurks like a big spider in the deep shade at the back of the produce stand beside the watermelons. A car pulls up. A woman gets out. She clutches her pocketbook nervously and squints into the shadows. She takes a few tentative steps.

"Idaho?" says Mr. Grange.

It's October. The flashing sign outside Mr. Grange's produce stand says:

YEA, THOUGH I WALK THROUGH THE
VALLEY OF THE SHADOW OF DEATH
I WILL FEAR NO EVIL
*pumpkins pomegranates persimmons
cane juice*

Mr. Grange likes to make decorations that reflect the season. Today he is making skeletons for Halloween. He cuts up bleached

149

gourds to be the skulls. He makes bones out of ash twigs and then wires them together. The finished skeletons flop around festively in the cool fall breeze under the eaves of the fruit stand. Mr. Grange's lap is full of bones. In the background there's the steady *clank clank* of the cane grinder, and a trickle of brown juice and scum flows from the spigot into gallon-size plastic jugs. Crocus sacks of pecans slump against each other in the middle of the floor. Pumpkins are piled up in every corner, and sheaves of sugarcane stalks and shocks of Indian corn lean against the wall.

Produce men stop by: apple men from the mountains, pecan men from the Piedmont, citrus men from central Florida. They stand around and talk produce and eat boiled peanuts. But Mr. Grange is taciturn. He silently bends ribs and drills holes in femurs with an auger.

By the end of October the last of the pumpkins is sold, and almost no one comes to the produce stand. Mr. Grange sits patiently in his aluminum chair out in the sun. He is philosophical. In Idaho, in the fall, everyone stays at home.

It's a cold gray day in February. The sign says:

THE LORD GIVETH
AND THE LORD TAKETH AWAY
BLESSED BE THE NAME OF THE LORD
collards   onions

Most of the shelves in the produce stand are bare. There are a few shriveled potatoes in the bottom of a bin and a couple of bundles of collard greens, bitten by the freeze. A bitter wind whips across the seared fields and bristly pastures behind the produce stand. Mr. Grange sits bundled up in his aluminum chair and cuts snowflakes out of lined notebook paper. He hangs the snowflakes from the rafters on lengths of baling twine. Another piece of notebook paper is taped to the wall with a message written in blue ballpoint pen: WINTER WONDERLAND.

I WILL LIFT UP MINE EYES UNTO THE HILLS
MY HELP COMETH FROM THE LORD
asparagus   jelly   rhubarb

In spring sugar snap peas glisten in their baskets, and bowls of mayhaws gleam like rubies. Mr. Grange has taken down the drooping snowflakes and is cutting bunnies out of freezer paper folded accordion-style. His big rough hands snip and snip — ears, a tail, back legs. Finally he stops cutting and separates the bunnies. The row spreads out, flops; he stretches it wide — and there they are, fifteen leaping bunnies, each with one hind foot connected to the front foot of the next bunny. But Mr. Grange doesn't smile. In his slow, workmanlike way he takes a pink crayon and colors a nose on every bunny.

A gentle breeze blows out of the west. In the field behind the produce stand the corn is up. The first peaches will soon be in. Mr. Grange gets out his big map and wipes off the dust. He gets out his box of tacks. He sets his aluminum chair out in the sun. And way across the land, across fields and woods and towns and rivers and lakes, in Idaho, the travelers begin to stir.

A Matter of Time

"We could be killed by this food," I whispered to Lilly.

She gingerly lifted up one edge of her cucumber slice and peered at the Ritz cracker underneath it. In the spirit of efficiency these little cucumber treats had been prepared that morning, and in the long hours sitting on the doily-lined platter, osmosis had been at work.

"I think you're supposed to put a dab of mayonnaise on the cracker to keep the moisture away," whispered Lilly.

"My God, don't mention mayonnaise!" I moaned. And indeed, this house looked like the birthplace of botulism — the dingy corners, the fusty Oriental rugs, a long-haired dog with a skin problem rubbing himself up against the furniture. In the kitchen a gummy knife lay on the counter, and the nubs of these very cucumbers were strewn around in the sink.

But it was a house of aesthetic significance, designed by our beloved and mysterious architect/craftsman, John Wind, who had come to town in the 1830s, built about ten exquisitely proportioned houses of unparalleled elegance in the Greek Revival style, and then disappeared without a trace.

Over the years, however, the demographics of the town have shifted, and some of those John Wind houses, once in the most fashionable parts of town, have ended up in neglected neighborhoods. The great avenues of live oaks meant to grace their approaches now just cast a damp shade. Mildew and mold grow on the peeling paint like gray fur. The shrubbery hedges, once clipped and trimmed, now rise up over the windows, and sills have rotted and plaster has cracked, and the elegant houses, with graffiti scrawled on the flush siding under the porches, slump and sink.

Miss Grantly poured lukewarm tea out of a silver teapot and then lolled back gracefully in her chair. A tuft of down pouffed out of a tiny hole in the cushion. I watched the little down threads as they rose and drifted toward us and surreptitiously covered my cucumber cracker with one hand.

"What is a person to do?" asked Miss Grantly.

But Miss Grantly was not a person who did things, so no one knew what to say.

We had been invited here because Lilly's brother Robert and his friend Peter Fielding were both architects and antiquarians with a deep interest in preserving significant landmarks, and Miss Grantly wanted advice about her deteriorating house. Six years ago she had begun stripping the blackened and crazed varnish off the interior woodwork. She had gone at it heroically for a week with rags and toothbrushes, but the little dentil blocks in the cornices and the flowerettes at the tops of the pilasters and the Greek key frets over the doors were too much for her. We could see where she had stopped; there were a couple of feet of golden, bare heart pine, then the thick black varnish again, and on the floor at that intersection the empty bottle of denatured alcohol, a couple of stiffened rags, a blackened toothbrush, and a pair of yellow rubber gloves still lay.

"You see," she said, waving her arm gracefully at the three-foot section of stripped cornice, "I do what I can."

Robert looked pained. He said, "Yes, but at this point it's more the structural things you need to worry about." He walked over to a corner of the room and stood for a minute, feeling the old house through his feet. Then he flexed his knees and bounced up and down. We felt the whole room sag and sway. A little wave of nausea crept over me. Miss Grantly daintily nibbled at her cracker.

"Yes, well, there's nothing I can do about *that,*" she said with relief.

That seemed to be the end of the visit. Lilly and I helped gather up the tea things and followed Miss Grantly back to the kitchen while Robert and Peter walked around in the four cluttered rooms and the wide central hall, stroking and thumping things, and reading the history of the house to each other in its surface and structure. Through the clatter of dishwashing we could hear their murmurs like voices at a wake.

At last Lilly and I got our coats and stood in the front hall saying good-bye to Miss Grantly. I could only think about the hair I felt lodged in the back of my throat, and wonder if it had come off Miss Grantly's own dog with the skin problem, or if it was an older hair, perhaps a hair from an ancestral dog, a dog from the turn of the century or earlier.

Lilly, in her helpful way, was nudging Miss Grantly into making a decision.

"There are those nice apartments on Gordon Avenue," she said hopefully.

Miss Grantly pinched and tweaked Lilly's arm thoughtfully with her soft little hands.

From under the house we heard some muffled taps and scraping. Robert and Peter were crawling around under there, poking sills and floor joists.

The dog rose from his corner of the sofa, stirring up a foul wind that hung in the air. He cocked his ears and growled.

"But do they allow pets?" Miss Grantly asked fretfully.

About a week later Lilly got a phone call in the middle of a rainy night. It was Miss Grantly, in tears. "Something has fallen on me!" she wailed. Lilly drove over there.

There was a leak in the roof, and the ceiling had finally collapsed. Miss Grantly stood in the middle of the room, surrounded by chunks and slabs of plaster and splintered lath, dirty water now streaming on the floor around her stringy white feet in their pink mules.

"These things happen," she said bravely. "Life is full of its little tribulations." Then she gathered up her dog, and a few things she might need, and went to stay with Lilly — "But only for a day or two. Just until something can be done, my dear," she said.

The next afternoon Lilly and I left school

early and hurried to Lilly's house to fix Miss Grantly a cup of tea. Miss Grantly's suitcase was sitting by the door, and she had her coat folded over her arm.

"Don't you worry, child," she told Lilly. "Everything will soon be put to right."

Then Lilly started in on the serious talk she had planned. "Miss Grantly, you know there's so much the house needs, so much more than you can do. And it's not safe for you to live there alone, what with the crime in your neighborhood. . . ." Miss Grantly's eyes began to fill with tears, and Lilly faltered. ". . . And things falling on you in the night. It may be time . . . you might want to consider . . . ," Lilly nervously poured out tea and rushed on, ". . . selling the house and . . ."

But Miss Grantly rose up in her chair and dabbed at her eyes. "Lilly," she said, "I'd sooner have it fall down around my ears than see strangers living in my house."

I pictured Miss Grantly with the house falling down around her ears. That was easy, since it had already begun to happen. But somehow I just couldn't picture the stranger who could stand to live in that house.

Then the door opened, letting in a cold, damp gust of wind, and Robert came in to give us the report. He was muddy and wet and smudged with the hundred-year-old coal dust that had settled in Miss Grantly's attic. He was not sanguine.

"Once the roof goes, it's just a matter of time," he said.

"A matter of time," mused Miss Grantly.

That weekend Lilly helped her select her best pieces of furniture and settled her into one of the apartments on Gordon Avenue. And once again we found ourselves sitting with Miss Grantly and her dog, drinking tea on a winter afternoon.

"Just until spring comes," Miss Grantly told us. "In the spring, things won't be falling in the night, and we'll move back home. You know," she added enigmatically, "these things have a way of fixing themselves."

"Well, yes," said Lilly, "but," she went on in a ringing tone, "by spring you may be feeling so comfortable here that — "

Miss Grantly cocked her head, raised her eyebrows, and waved a finger in the air. "It's just a matter of time," she said.

Sam Martin made his back cut; then he stood and looked up into the top of the big old tree. It stood graceful and silent for a few seconds, there were some deep cracks, then with a slow whooshing sound it came down and hit with a thump Sam could feel through his feet and up to his chest. The clean smell of pine tar rose in the air, and Sam began counting rings. For a few easy years, the early years, the tree had grown fast, and the rings were wide and soft. Then for a hundred years or so they had tightened up, and Sam had to squint and blink to count them. Then, about fifty years ago the rings had spread out wide again. Sam straightened up and looked at the longleaf pinewoods around him. Probably the surrounding trees had gone down in the hurricane of 1941, he thought, and then this old tree got a new lease on life.

He dug the tongs into the butt end of the tree, raised the hitch on the tractor, and snaked the twenty-foot butt log through the woods to the Wood Mizer.

Sam loved machines, but of all the machines he had known through the years, this sawmill was his favorite. With the cant hooks Sam shoved and rolled the log onto the loaders, then pulled a lever at the front end of the mill, and the loaders rose up and rolled the log onto the bed. Sam oiled the chain and the guide rails. He greased the guide bearings and adjusted the blade tensioner. Then he measured from the heart out at both ends of the log and raised the toe board at the top end so the cut would be parallel to the heart. Then he lowered the blade, and slowly and gently the cutting head moved down the log. When it got to the end, Sam dragged the slab off, turned the log, measured again, adjusted the toe boards up and down, then ran the head back and made another cut. This time there was a two-inch board with bark on both sides — a flitch. Sam flipped it off, turned the log, measured again, and cut off another slab and another flitch.

Sam measured and cut and flipped boards off the log until he was left with an eight-by-fourteen-inch sill on the bed of his sawmill. On the right was a pile of slabs and boards, and on the left, a faint trail of the sawdust that had spewed out a little chute as the blade moved down the log. That was the only difference between a tree standing in the woods with a story to tell and a floor sill for some old house, Sam thought. Wood Mizer. Good name for it.

"I'm cutting out in some old virgin woods," he told his wife that night. "Way out there from Reno. Peter Fielding's old place. They want real boxed heart sills, not laminated. And fifteen-hundred feet of quartersawn five-quarter flooring. Don't get much orders for five quarter, particularly quartersawn." He

161

shook his head. "It's gon' cost 'em. Must be gon' be something nice."

That night there were sounds in Miss Grantly's house: the rattle of tape measures and muffled voices and the steady rasp of a saw in the kitchen. Now and then the gleam of a flashlight would wink out through the shrubbery. The next night a big truck pulled into the overgrown pecan orchard behind the house. And in the morning Miss Grantly's house was gone.

"Gone, gone," she whimpered, standing in her pink mules in the dust and doodlebugs where her house had been and twisting and untwisting a corner of her fringed shawl. At the back of the lot the kitchen wing still stood, tipped forward slightly. The sawed off ends of its siding boards gleamed bright in the morning sun, and the cabinet doors swung open. Lilly stood beside Miss Grantly, her arm around her thin shoulders, and we looked around at all the junk that had been thrown under Miss Grantly's house over the past 150 years. I kept wanting to poke around in it, like a child discovering undersea treasures revealed by a receding tide, but we seemed to be in the middle of one of those reverent moments of silence, so I stood still and watched a homeless spider crawling testily over the headlamp of a Model A Ford.

Back at Lilly's house we settled Miss Grantly in the living room and made a fuss over her. Lilly made her some cinnamon toast drenched with butter, and I picked her a bunch of poppies.

"These young people today," Miss Grantly sighed, dabbing at her last tear and sinking down luxuriously into Lilly's gold damask sofa, "such rogues they are. They stole my car, they stole my television, they stole Mother's jewelry. It was just a matter of time," she said with a satisfied smack, "until they stole the whole house."

"All except the kitchen," I added cheerfully, but Lilly glared at me, and we ate our cinnamon toast in silence.

After that Miss Grantly seemed to rally. She settled down very peacefully in the Gordon Avenue apartments. It was a civilized place, a Victorian brick building in the Gothic Revival style, with tall windows in every room, and carefully tended grounds with neat brick walkways winding through beds of trimmed azaleas. Lilly talked Miss Grantly into using their weekly cleaning service, and, removed from the stench and squalor of a century and a half of bad housekeeping, she became more accessible and made good friends among her neighbors. When she could no longer manage the stairs, she moved down to a ground-floor apartment. A year after that, her dog died. Miss Grantly began to rely more and more on the story of her house for comfort and attention.

"My house was stolen," she would say over and over, "stolen clean away — except the kitchen, of course, a 1910 addition." Then she would lay her hand on the arm of her listener and add with a little flourish, "It was a John Wind house, of course."

In the spring of her ninety-third year, Miss Grantly died in her sleep. She had no family, and Lilly arranged the funeral. There was the fragrance of wild azalea and rosemary, and over the strains of "Sheep May Safely Graze" muted snatches of conversation could be heard:

". . . such a sweet old lady."

"dreadful old house . . ."

"what a blessing . . ."

". . . stolen . . ."

"died so peacefully"

"you know her house was stolen . . ."

". . . John Wind . . ."

". . . then . . . stolen"

"dear Lilly"

". . . except the kitchen, a 1910 addition"

"what a saint"

A week later Lilly had a little dinner party at her house. It was just me, and Robert and Peter, but Lilly wore her black silk dress, and everything was elegantly done. When we had finished eating and Lilly had folded her napkin, Robert and Peter stood up. "Come and take a little drive with us," Peter said.

We drove through town and into the country. We drove way out past Reno, to the old Fielding place. Robert opened a gate, and we drove through a pasture, over a hill, and into an old stand of longleaf pine trees. Through the pines I could see an elegantly proportioned Greek Revival cottage, with slender square columns, flat jigsawed porch balusters in a sheaf of wheat design, and the John Wind signature oak leaf medallion in the pediment. The double doors were open, and the old dimpled glass in the sidelights and transom winked and twinkled in the low evening light.

The interior woodwork had been stripped bare, and the dentiled cornices, the fluted pilasters, and the Greek key fretwork over the doors glowed a rich, smooth gold. Here and there on the floor I could see where new quartersawn floorboards had been fitted.

I walked slowly from the front of the hall to the back. Everything was level and true. Everywhere was the clean, sharp smell of pine.

Lilly stood at the window in the front room with her hands clasped behind her back, looking down into the woods. In the middle of the room was the one piece of furniture in the house, a delicate tiger-maple Queen Anne tea table with cabriole legs. On the table were a bottle of wine and four glasses. Peter poured out the wine and handed it around to us. Lilly smiled then, and Robert raised his glass to her and said, "It was only a matter of time."

Garden of Eden

I know some people who believe that God created Adam and Eve one mile east of Bristol, Florida, on the Florida panhandle, and that the Garden of Eden was located in Torreya State Park just north of Bristol, and that Noah built the ark right near the intersection of state road 12 and I-10 out of the wood of the now-endangered Torreya tree, also called Stinking Cedar, which grows nowhere else in the world.

The book of Genesis says, "a river went out of Eden to water the garden; and from thence it was parted, and became into four heads." There's only one place on earth where four rivers come together, and that's near Bristol, Florida.

God told Noah, "Make thee an ark of gopher wood." The Torreya tree, an ancient and primitive species, has another name besides stinking cedar: locals call it gopher wood. When the flood came, so they say, the ark floated all the way from Bristol halfway around the world to Mt. Ararat, and Noah and his dazed family climbed out into a strange land, with nothing left but stories of their lost homeland in north Florida.

A lot of people around Bristol believe this, and if you show any inclination to listen, they will go on to tell you that twenty-eight species of trees are mentioned in the Bible, and that more of those twenty-eight occur near Bristol, Florida, than anywhere else on earth, and that within the limestone formations in that area have been found the fossilized remains of every animal ever known to have lived. If your attention begins to wander, they'll throw in a few wild facts about gold up the Chattahoochee, onyx, and the skeletons of giants.

Arrive early in the morning on a summer day at Torreya State Park for a day's hiking, and no matter how skeptical you are, for just a moment, right at dawn, you will almost believe you are in the Garden of Eden. You can sit in a cool breeze on a high bluff overlooking one of the four rivers and admire your new two-tone hiking boots and special moisture-wicking socks, and gaze down a long view into the mist, and smell the sweetness in the air, and think about all things bright and beautiful, all creatures great and small.

But by noon the mist has burned off and has been replaced by a kind of pulsating haze that seems to amplify the heat, and you realize that 90 percent of those fossilized animals in the limestone have living descendants, and that most of those have bitten or stung you. You begin to wonder which of the six species of serpents you have nimbly avoided in the cypress sloughs and hardwood hammocks was the one that offered Eve the fruit of the knowledge of good and evil.

By midafternoon, you have discovered a dark cloud of millions of tiny ticks seeping like a stain up your pant leg, you have eaten all the trail mix out of your little pouch, and you feel like you'd give anything for an apple, no matter who offered it, and you'd sell your soul and Adam's too for a drink of ice water. Sweat and duckweed have formed a quagmire inside your new hiking boots, the moisture-wicking fibers in your socks have collapsed into the slurry, and there seems to be a sort of atmospheric poison ivy that is causing all your exposed skin to break out in little itchy red blisters.

When the sun begins to go down, the no-see-ums come out and bite you in every place the mosquitoes can't reach. When it gets dark, you turn on your flashlight, and in the path ahead of you the yellow eyes of giant spiders glow, and mosquito hawks the size of praying mantises drift around your head, and you decide that despite the fossil evidence and the four rivers and the gopher wood, this place is none other than Hell on Earth.

At last, covered with briar scratches, chiggers, and ticks, your clothes in tatters and your feet pickled in their own sweat, you emerge from the woods. You apologize to the irritated park ranger in his neat tan uniform who snarls, "We close at dusk," and you stagger across the parking lot to your car, knowing more about good and evil than you ever dreamed you'd be able to find out just north of Bristol in the Florida panhandle on one summer day.

CLOSE TO HOME

The Wedding Guest

There I was at a wedding reception, sitting in a chair against the wall, and trying to keep my feet out of sight, because I was wearing purple sandals and I had suddenly decided that my feet looked big and strange.

An old woman hobbled over and carefully lowered herself into the chair beside me. She planted the rubber tip of her walking stick on the floor between her two feet and piled her hands on the handle. She gave me a sharp look.

"I believe I knew your grandmother," she said.

The handle of her walking stick was shaped like a dragon's head, with a jade nose and ivory fangs. Its ebony lips were curled into a snarl, and its ruby eyes glared fiercely up at me between her gnarly fingers.

"A dreadful woman," she said.

I tucked my feet farther under my chair

and tried to think of something to say.

"So unbecoming," she went on, "that enthusiasm she had for polo."

"What an interesting walking stick that is," I said. "I have seen horse-head walking sticks and dog-head walking sticks, but I don't believe I've ever seen a dragon-head walking stick."

She reared back, pulled her glasses down her nose, and looked at me over the top of them.

"Are you quite sane?" she asked.

"Well," I said, "I've always felt myself to be . . ." The little red eyes of the dragon seemed to wink and twinkle. ". . . until . . ."

"Amazing," she said. "Such a very odd family."

"But oddness is not a genetic taint," I said defensively.

"Take a look at this walking stick," she said, seizing the dragon by the throat and thrusting its open mouth at my face. "What would you say that is?"

Rattling around in the dragon's maw, fenced in by the ivory teeth, was a blue lump of something that looked like chewing gum. "Turquoise?" I guessed.

"Chewing gum!" she crowed. "Blue chewing gum chewed by the jeweler himself and installed as a replacement for the turquoise bead that flew out and was permanently lost under my sofa." And with a sharp smack she planted the tip of the walking stick back on the floor.

"Are you a friend of the bride's family or the groom's family?" I asked.

"So foolish of young people to marry today," she said. "Much better to just stay at home — simpler and more hygienic."

I demurred.

"Now why are you sitting here talking to me, when you should be out there drinking punch and joining into this scintillating chatter we hear about us?"

Oh well, I thought, and I plunged right in: "Because I am embarrassed by these giant purple sandals, and I feel that my feet look big and strange." Slowly I brought my feet out from under the chair. She peered down at them.

"Whoo!" she said, "quite right too. They look like something that might have escaped from a traveling menagerie."

"I thought I would just sit here until people start to leave," I said. "Then maybe I will be able to creep out."

"Yes," she said, "sidling along the wall like a stealthy roach that doesn't realize it has already been spotted."

"Something like that," I said.

We sat for a while in silence, looking over the room of happy wedding guests, she with her walking stick, I with my purple shoes. At last she turned to me.

"In general I do not like talking to young people," she said. "But I have so enjoyed talking to you."

And she clutched the dragon by the head, thrust herself up out of the chair, tweaked her skirt smooth, and was gone.

Career Choices

When I was a young woman I wanted more than anything else to be a nurse. I imagined myself traveling the world, giving succor wherever there was pain and suffering. Sickly babies would smile and grow fat in my arms, old dying Biafrans would rise from their foul straw pallets and walk after my ministrations, and victims of railway accidents, swathed in bandages and wired up in traction, would find a strange comfort in their delirium at the sound of my feet coming down the hall in their great white shoes.

When I went to college, I signed up for the four-year nursing program. I breezed right through the first two years of pure science courses. Photosynthesis seemed as natural as breathing, and meiosis and mitosis were like two little kid brothers of mine whose antics I'd been watching since childhood. It was a thorough and satisfying beginning to my life's work.

Then finally, in the third year, my classmates and I were sent out to a hospital for the first time, proudly wearing our little caps and white stockings and the gray pinstriped uniform of the fledgling nurse.

It wasn't like I expected. Instead of that mystical power of healing that I had imagined would enter me like a great bird, I felt all my good sense drain away, and the useless weight of the pain and suffering of all those thousands of souls settled in my belly like a lead-gray stone.

At the end of three months' work in the hospital, our nursing supervisor had a conference with each of us to evaluate our performance. Mine did not go well. She said she would be frank with me. "In all my years here as nursing supervisor," she said, "I have never seen such incompetence in a student nurse." The tears streamed down my face, and I needed to blow my nose. "I'm sorry," she said, "I don't have a Kleenex." Then she walked me to the door. "Why don't you take a year off?" she said. "Think about what you really want to do with your life."

That afternoon I went up to the school's administration building and withdrew my records. The next day I got a job as a waitress in a twenty-four-hour restaurant called Our Place Your Eating Pleasure. I was not a great waitress, but I was neat and clean. I was always on time, and I worked hard. I washed dishes, set tables, and served breakfast, lunch, and supper from eleven at night until dawn. And during the long nights, carrying plates of scrambled eggs and country-fried steak to the weary customers, I would think about my failed career and wonder what I would do with my life. Outside the neon sign blinked on and off to display OUR PLACE alternately with YOUR EATING PLEASURE.

One night I overheard Stanley, the manager, and Marge, the head waitress, talking about me. "She's a nice kid, but she's not P.I.C. material," Stanley said. P.I.C. meant "person in charge." Several of the more capable waitresses and cooks at Our Place Your Eating Pleasure were designated P.I.C.'s. It came as no surprise to me that Stanley did not consider me to be P.I.C. material. After all, I kept telling myself, in all her years the nursing supervisor had never seen such incompetence in a student nurse.

After I had been working at Our Place Your Eating Pleasure for several weeks, a new employee came to the restaurant. He was a Sockett from south Alabama, but his

179

mother had come from a "better" family, the Nockerds, from east Tennessee. Out of pride she had given her little son her family name, so he was named Nockerd Sockett. He was round and fat, he had an energetic gait, a bright, lively face, and laughing eyes.

As soon as Nockerd Sockett got there, things began to change at Our Place Your Eating Pleasure. He started by moving the stack of napkins over by the knives and forks so we didn't have to cross the room to get a place setting. He moved the anchovies to the end of the steam table so they wouldn't drip into the lima beans. He bought a used glass-washing machine and fixed it up so the brush would spin again.

Then he went to work on the minds of the Our Place Your Eating Pleasure customers. He came in one Monday morning and painted all the counters and cabinets gloss white, because "white is a symbol of cleanliness," he said. He borrowed a sewing machine and stitched up little curtains for the windows from fabric printed with pictures of fruits and vegetables "to put people in an eating mood," he said. Everything began to feel smooth and easy at Our Place Your Eating Pleasure. It was clear that Nockerd Sockett was just born to be a P.I.C.

With all the improvements in personnel

efficiency, we sometimes ended up in those dreary predawn hours with nothing to do, and we would sit down at one of the tables and drink coffee and talk. There would be me, and Marge, who you'd think from her shape alone was the *Venus of Willendorf*, except that her little pin said HI! MY NAME IS: Marge. There was April, the frail little artist who was studying to be a glassblower; there was Cindi, the slinky, sultry girl who worked Tuesdays and Thursdays at the Flamingo Lounge next door; and there was Nockerd Sockett.

Marge would mother us all and make strange sandwiches for us to eat, Cindi would slouch seductively in her chair and fling her hair around from shoulder to shoulder, and April would open up her fringed leather bag and pull out her latest creations in glass. At first she could only make chunky, thick, hollow vessels, with nasty colored drools down the sides; they looked like they might be bud vases for skunk cabbages. But with time her glass took on more grace and style, and toward the end of my year at Our Place Your Eating Pleasure she would pull out of her leather bag lovely, clear, thin globes, with the faintest tint of iridescence when they turned in the light. I would sit and wipe the grease off the salt and pepper shakers with a soapy rag and think about all the lives I would never save, and Nockerd would tell us stories about his childhood in south Alabama.

Nockerd Sockett had not had an easy life. His father, one of those sorry south Alabama Socketts, had abandoned the family when Nockerd was just an infant. Nockerd had been twelve years old before he owned his first pair of shoes. He and his sisters had some rabbits in a hutch in the backyard, and sometimes they would come home from school to find one of their pets missing. They would search the woods behind the house, and Nockerd would tack the chicken wire tighter around the cage. That night for the first time in months, their mother would put meat on the table, something not quite like chicken.

Nockerd had married his childhood sweetheart when he was sixteen years old, and within a year she had a baby boy with a dreadful birth defect and ran off with another man. Nockerd was left with the little baby, who died a pitiful death before he was two. Nockerd would tell us these stories, but then he would smile his cheerful smile and say, "I got nowhere to go but up, and ladies, I'm on my way!"

For some reason, in spite of my lugubrious

mood and dark musings about my failed life's mission, Nockerd took a liking to me. He would do little things to make my work easier at Our Place Your Eating Pleasure, and sometimes he would give me a great hug and a smacking kiss on the cheek, and announce, "We're in love. She just don't know it yet." But that year, what with the lives not saved, and not being P.I.C. material, I was not in the mood for love.

On Christmas Eve, Nockerd and Cindi took the night off to go to a big party at the Flamingo Lounge, but Nockerd came by Our Place Your Eating Pleasure to give us our presents, and to say Merry Christmas. It was a gray, wet, mean winter evening, but when Nockerd came out of the gloom from between the two Dumpsters and in the back door, it was like the strangest spring on earth had come into that room. He was dressed in a purple imitation suede coat with a fringe of matted fake fur at the hem that looked like a row of dead pink rats that had been left out in the rain. He had on a shiny mauve polyester shirt and lavender high-heeled tooled leather cowboy boots, and his toes turned out so cheerfully, and his little plump hands thrusting out of the pink fur cuffs of that coat were the happiest hands I'd ever seen. My face had almost forgotten how to smile, but when Nockerd spread his arms out and made a slow twirl so we could get the full effect of his Christmas outfit, I laughed out loud for the first time in six months.

But with the new year and the lengthening days, things began to go wrong at Our Place Your Eating Pleasure. Stanley, the manager, resented Nockerd's meddling ways. He wanted to be the big boss at Our Place Your Eating Pleasure. He wanted to be the one who did the organizing and made the improvements. Strange things began to happen. One day Nockerd came to work and found tomato sauce poured all over the floor in the cooler. Another day six bags of flour had been slashed open.

Then, one day in April, money was found missing. The records for the past weeks were examined. More money was not accounted for. Nockerd, as P.I.C. for the late shift, had the job of closing out the cash register every night. So the auditors called him in to ask him questions.

"I didn't steal that money," Nockerd said over and over. "I may be a Sockett, but I'm not a criminal. I didn't steal that money."

We didn't hear these things firsthand, but we knew enough to realize that that night would be Nockerd's last at Our Place Your

Eating Pleasure. Nobody knew what to say. Marge's lips were tight, and her bosom was heaving. She loved Nockerd, but she was a decent, law-abiding woman. "He has sunk," she muttered under her breath. "He has sunk to this." April, who worked the afternoon shift that day, pressed into Nockerd's hand a tiny little glass bird with exquisite pink feet, whispered a trembling "Good-bye!" and then fled sobbing to the parking lot. Cindi, who perhaps knew Nockerd better than the rest of us, kept her silence and slouched desultorily from table to table wiping swirls on the plastic wood grain with a greasy rag. But Nockerd just looked out over the floor of the restaurant where the diners were gathering for supper, and said, "Watch this."

Having been stripped of his P.I.C. status, he was just a waiter that night. But "Watch this," he said, and we did. We couldn't help it. It was like there was a contest between Nockerd Sockett and the best waiters from all the finest restaurants in the whole world, and Nockerd Sockett was winning. It was like he had a dozen hands and winged feet. One second he would be pouring coffee in one corner of the room, and the next second he would be serving desserts and giving directions to the airport in the other corner. He waited on a table of fifteen men from the Snap-On Tools convention who all wanted different salad dressings and more of this and less of that; Nockerd never made a single mark on his pad, and he never made a single mistake. Everyone's check appeared on the table one instant before they realized they were ready to go, and those who wanted to linger over their coffee found their dirty dishes silently whisked away, and in their place a new napkin, a gleaming spoon, and sugar and cream appeared on the sparkling tabletop.

As the night went by, a feeling grew in that room of peace and contentment and satisfaction and joy. The conversations of the diners fell to a low murmur, like the flutings of doves, and they leaned over the tables and looked at each other with sweet faces. Something about the air was changed, so that the colors of things seemed to glow with their own light, and the water in the glasses sparkled and twinkled, and there was a smell of lemons and rosemary. Through it all Nockerd worked, carrying four plates on each arm, spinning a round tray of water glasses slowly over his head, and giving all the diners exactly what they wanted. "Watch," he told us. "Watch this." It was like Nockerd was performing an exquisite dance, right there on the floor of Our Place Your Eating

Pleasure, and all the people eating their supper and drinking their coffee were a part of the dance, and the flashing neon light outside was keeping time to beautiful music that we could not quite hear.

After that night, Nockerd was gone. We never saw him again at Our Place Your Eating Pleasure. And soon, my "year off" was over. "Those who can, do, and those who can't, teach," I'd heard all my life, so there seemed to be only one career choice open for me. I went back to college and entered the School of Education. I became a first-grade teacher, and after twenty years in the classroom I almost forgot about my youthful desire to be a nurse and my year at Our Place Your Eating Pleasure.

Then one day at school, a little girl ran up to me. "Miss White, Miss White, Thomas swallowed twenty-five cents!" And sure enough, there was Thomas in the reading corner, soundlessly turning blue and clutching at his throat. In one instant I grabbed him under the chest, put my fist in position just below his sternum, and gave the thrust — once, twice, three times — and out flew, not a shiny quarter with George Washington's smug smile, as I had expected, but two dimes and a nickel.

That afternoon in the grocery store parking

lot I saw a man unloading frozen turkeys from a refrigerator truck. I went closer. I knew I'd seen that man before. But you can't just walk up to someone who may very well be a total stranger and ask, "Is your name Nockerd Sockett?"

I'll just say his name, I thought. If it's Nockerd, he'll turn and look.

I stood in the middle of the parking lot. "Nockerd!" I called out. "Nockerd Sockett!"

The man on the truck stopped, a frozen turkey in his arms. He turned to look at me. But then so did everybody else in the parking lot. I walked over to the truck. It was a cold November day, but I felt the air grow hot and still around my face. My ears began to ring.

The man on the truck looked down at me with the saddest eyes I'd ever seen. He took a step backward.

"Nockerd," I said, "it's me! Remember Our Place Your Eating Pleasure, Marge, the little glass bird with pink feet, the lavender cowboy suit?" I took a step closer. "I'm a teacher, Nockerd. I've taught hundreds of children to read and write and count money. Today I saved a life. It's almost like I've become a P.I.C. after all these years."

But he just threw the turkey into the bin and turned to get another one. He looked back at me one last time and shook his head. Inside the truck I could see what looked like a thousand frozen turkeys stacked up like a pile of stones. And tomorrow would be Thanksgiving.

Dr. Fielding

There is something quite comforting about being given a complete physical examination by a beloved old family doctor, now nearly blind. I sat up on the table in the little tissue-paper gown, and Dr. Fielding asked about my different body parts as if they were old friends of his. Looking down at myself, I hardly recognized those two pink knees. They looked like some old lady's knees. And those ghastly feet, all strings and knobs, dangling halfway to the floor, looked like feet I'd never seen.

But Dr. Fielding took those feet up in his two warm hands and asked, "How about this old broken toe? Does it ache in cold weather?"

"Why, yes, it does," I said.

"And you've abused your knees with all that gardening, you know. You need to watch that squatting and kneeling now."

Then he turned, and before he could even open the drawer where he keeps his little rubber mallet, my feet both flew up and kicked out, so eager were my reflexes to please Dr. Fielding. He made me close my eyes to ensure a more reasonable reaction before he gave each knee its official tap.

We went into his office, then, for the last part of the visit, the part where I sit in the chrome-handled chair beside his desk and stare at the dusty old model skeleton and tell Dr. Fielding what's on my mind. The skeleton used to scare me when I was a little girl and my feet didn't touch the floor in this chair. But Dr. Fielding knows that it's easier to tell your troubles to a rack of bones than to a living person with flesh and blood, and staring into those dusty eye sockets I've told Dr. Fielding all kinds of things over the years, from the bizarre anxieties of adolescence to the odd delusions I had in my early twenties that I was suffering from nineteenth-century diseases.

"I have this little dry hacking cough. There's no blood in the handkerchief yet, but I wonder, could it be . . . consumption?"

And a month later, meeting the skeleton's gaze quite bravely, I began, "This rash, and a little fever . . ."

"What do you think?" asked Dr. Fielding.

"The pox," I whispered.

Then dizzy spells, insomnia, night sweats. "Brain fever?"

But Dr. Fielding didn't answer me. Instead he asked a question. "Do you ever read twentieth-century literature? I hear that fellow John O'Hara's pretty good. You go on home now, and put those Victorian novels away. Come see me in a week if you don't feel better."

But on this visit I had a real problem to discuss with Dr. Fielding. Failing eyesight was forcing him to retire. This was to be his last week in his office. The skeleton had come unhinged in several crucial joints and slumped disconsolately. Its head sagged, and it could not meet my gaze. "Who will be my doctor now?"

Dr. Fielding took out a list of all the new physicians in town and checked off several names. I recognized one.

"But I taught that child in first grade!" I moaned.

Another one, I happened to know, was comfortingly middle-aged, but he had moved here from New York and had a ponytail and drove a red Porsche. Several of the doctors on the list were women. Most were specialists of one kind or another.

In the end, Dr. Fielding put my records

in my hands, a bundle of yellow cards and folded sheets of paper held together with a rubber band. He gave me a pat and a shove. "You'll be fine," he said.

But when I got out to the waiting room, my legs wouldn't walk any farther. I sat down on the cracked vinyl sofa. All my body parts felt like lumps of lead. I tried to reason with them. I wheedled and pleaded. I told my uterus, "Don't worry, I'll find you a new doctor, a real gynecologist. Maybe a nice lady gynecologist, who understands the special needs of women." But my uterus had gone into a kind of blue funk and did not respond.

I told my knees, "We'll get a joint specialist, an orthopedist who does laser surgery." But my knees just glared balefully into the distance. I felt a twinge of pain.

"For you," I told my skin, "a dermatologist, with a Latin name for every itch.

"And a therapist!" I told my brain, "a psychotherapist licensed by the state! He'll read all the magazines and keep up with the latest neuroses." But all my emotions just huddled in my head in a sodden mass and sulked.

I began to understand. My whole body, having been treated by me all these years with nothing but suspicion and abuse, now wanted to abandon me and stay here with its old friend Dr. Fielding, sending what's left of me, a little zephyr of consciousness, out the door and into the swirling beyond. I sat for a while and thought about it. I took a deep breath. I drew myself up. Then I took a stand. After all, who was the boss here?

"You are behaving like spoiled two-year-olds," I told my body parts. "Now get yourselves out that door."

And they did. We all stepped out together and stood on the porch of Dr. Fielding's office for the last time. There was the old familiar smell of the oak tree shade. A red Porsche glided down the street. It was a convertible. The top was down. The doctor from New York's ponytail blew in the breeze. He gave me a confident smirk of a grin. He waved. For a second I just stood there.

"You wave, sirrah!" I commanded my arm.

And reluctantly, but obediently, my arm rose, my hand dipped once, up and down. I greeted my new doctor.

Vanishing Species

Many years ago a man came down here with a whole station wagon full of recording equipment. He was on a quest to acquire and preserve amazing and unusual natural sounds from all over the world. He had just been in the South Seas recording Tasmanian devils, and somewhere he had heard about my aunt Belle's alligator, the one she had trained to bellow on command.

This was back in the days when alligators had been hunted to the brink of extinction, and people believed that their bellow, one of the most truly majestic of all animal sounds, might soon be lost forever.

My aunt loaded Mr. Linley and all his recording equipment into her pickup truck and backed him down to the edge of the pond where the alligator lived. Then she revved up the engine a couple of times, and pretty soon here came the alligator.

We hadn't been too impressed with Mr. Linley at first. He just seemed like a quiet, pale little man with quick-moving hands and a nervous flicker in his eyes. But when that alligator came crawling up out of the mud, Mr. Linley slung his tape recorder over his shoulder, plugged in a bunch of black cables, pressed RECORD, then vaulted out of the truck and went crawling down the bank to meet him. We'd never seen anyone do that before. My aunt's alligator ate things that came out of the back of that truck. He ate everything that came out of the back of that truck. But we didn't want to be recorded, so we didn't say anything.

Aunt Belle revved the engine a few more times then shut it off. A quail bird whistled. The hot engine ticked. Then we saw the alligator swell up. Mr. Linley stuck out a microphone as long as his arm, right up to those ragged jaws. The alligator slumped down in the middle, we saw the water begin to quiver around his jowls, and the bellowing began. It went on for a full two minutes. Mr. Linley didn't flinch. He held that microphone steady with all his heart.

When it ended, Mr. Linley and the alligator moved at the same time. Mr. Linley made it into the back of the truck in two leaps, but it seemed like that alligator almost took

196

flight. He crashed into the tailgate just as Mr. Linley crashed into the back of the cab. The alligator left a big dent in the tailgate, with teeth marks scraped through the paint, and Mr. Linley left a shiny smear down the back of the cab where he rubbed the dust off as he slumped down.

We were impressed. Now we understood that nervous flicker in Mr. Linley's eyes and those quivering hands.

And now that it was all over, Mr. Linley became quite garrulous. He sat down on our porch and eagerly showed us how his equipment worked. He played back the alligator bellowing. It was amazing. It was better than the real thing. You could hear drops of water fall from the alligator's top teeth into the muddy puddle that swirled around his bottom jaw. You could hear that little pink flap of skin at the back of his throat open up. You could hear time and distance. You could hear silence.

Then Mr. Linley played some of his other recordings for us. He played star-nosed moles snuffling on a moonlight night. He played an almost extinct worm crawling through dead leaves. He played whales, he played sharks, he played icebergs groaning.

But when he started playing his recording of Viennese cats mating, our dog began to howl. He was an old bird dog, tied up to his doghouse in the backyard, and he really began to do some fancy howling. It was almost like a yodel. Mr. Linley got excited.

"I've never heard a dog do that," he said.

And quick as a flash he whipped out his unidirectional microphone. The dog howled, the little needle jumped up into the red, and Mr. Linley did his work.

After a few minutes the dog shut up. Mr. Linley began dismantling his equipment. He unplugged the cables, shoved all the levers over to the far left, and rewound the tape. Then he stopped. His hands stopped trembling. His eyes grew steady. He didn't breathe. Something was wrong. He had erased his alligator recording. He had taped the howling dog right over it.

So back we went to the edge of the pond; back Mr. Linley crawled into the mud. My aunt revved and revved the engine. But the alligator just lay there, eye to eye with Mr. Linley. He didn't raise up his tail. He didn't raise up his head. He didn't slump down in the middle. Water didn't quiver around his jowls. He just lay silent in the mud and glared at Mr. Linley.

Finally we drove back home. Mr. Linley packed up his equipment, bid us a desultory good-bye, and went off to record the courtship rituals of the Komodo dragon. We never heard from him again.

Since then, laws protecting alligators have resulted in a resurgence in their population. They have been removed from the endangered species list. And almost any summer night in any southern swamp or river or pond you can hear alligators bellowing. We're not worried about them anymore. But I sometimes wonder whatever happened to that little Mr. Linley.

The Retired Russian Colonel

During the last week in May our principal announced that a retired Russian colonel would be visiting our school and that she would like for the first-grade classes to present their end-of-school musical program for him. Since our auditorium had just been torn up as part of an extensive remodeling project, the performance would have to take place on the playground with the children standing in the dirt, the piano wobbling on a grassy knoll, and the retired Russian colonel sitting in a little red chair under the pecan tree.

This would be the third time the children had performed this program — once for the PTO, once for the rest of the school, and now for the Russian colonel. Enthusiasm was not high. "Behave yourselves," I warned my students. "Little Russian children are always well behaved."

But the performance did not go well. What

with cars going by on the street, birds singing, and the batteries being dead on the battery-powered microphone, the whole thing was barely audible. The children began to misbehave. There was pushing and jostling, faces were made, and at one point Miss Meadows actually had to go up and speak to one of the performers. Still, the Russian colonel sat attentively in his chair in his trim olive green uniform, his white hair bright in the sun and a cheerful look on his little pink face. At one point he took a pad out of his pocket and made a note with a tiny pencil. "Do you think he's a spy?" Miss Meadows whispered to me.

Finally it ended, and we filed back to our classrooms where we sat the children down and lectured them about duty, responsibility, and important foreign dignitaries. Later in the day we all assembled in the library, and the retired Russian colonel gave the first graders a little talk about life in Russia. First he held up snapshots of family members and scenes of Moscow. At that distance all we could see were bits of color and gloss. But the children were forgiving. After all, the colonel had not been able to hear their musical program.

He taught them to count to ten in Russian, and then he said, "I liked very much your

singing this morning. I too enjoy singing."
And with that he clasped both hands gently
over his chest and burst into song. There
was a moment of stunned silence, but before
long, with many winks and welcoming ges-
tures, he had the children singing along. The
song, he explained afterward, was "Kalinka,
Kalinka" and told all about a tree with red
fruit.

Then he took out one of those dolls, each
piece of which unscrews to reveal a smaller
doll within. The children greeted each new
doll with riotous pleasure and were most
delighted of all when he demonstrated with
a magnificently misleading flourish that the
last pea-sized doll did not open up. "Do it
again!" someone begged. But he lined the
dolls up neatly in their order on top of the
bookcase and said, "You would not receive
such pleasure a second time."

Then, with the teachers' guidance, the children asked their prepared questions: "What
kind of public transportation do you have
in Russia?" and "What is a typical school
day like for a Russian first grader?" But
after a while the prepared questions were
used up, and the dreaded spontaneous questions began. "What do you eat in Russia?"
"How old are you?" and "How much money
do you make?" The answers were cheerfully

given: Potatoes and something called fruit compote, seventy-five, and an astounding number of rubles.

"And now," he said to the children, "You may be wondering to what I attribute my trim shape and good physical condition." I had been wondering that, and also to what he attributed his charm and good nature.

"I jog," he said, and we nodded approvingly, "and," he went on, "I am a winter bather." Every winter day, he explained, he marches right down to the Volga River, chops a hole in the ice, and plunges in. This winter bathing, he told us, together with moderate eating and exercise, is the key to vigor and health. He advised the first graders to begin at once by turning off the hot water in the shower and standing in the cold stream, the first day for four seconds, the next day for ten seconds, and so on. And with that advice he concluded his presentation, and we went back to our classrooms.

That afternoon the children wrote their daily journal entries. "May 31, 1993," wrote one little boy. "When I grow up, I want to be a retired Russian colonel."

An Old Lepidopterist

One summer when I was a little girl, an old lepidopterist rented a cabin in the woods up the road from us. He moved down from Atlanta with his tiny, perfectly round wife, and a station wagon full of nets, spreading boards, and killing jars. He was finishing up his life's work, an exhaustive study of the butterflies of Georgia, and he was, we learned later, an eminently respected and renowned scientist in his field. But to the children in my neighborhood that summer, he was just a very kind old man with a lot of interesting stuff on his back porch, which he was happy to show off and explain to us.

His wife was a great homemaker and needle-worker, and as soon as she had settled in and sent Mr. Harris off into the pine woods with his butterfly net and two pimento cheese sandwiches, she began baking exquisite little cookies and knitting little pink sweaters for me and all my cousins.

In the late afternoons of that summer, when it began to cool off, Mr. Harris would come back with his jar full of buckeyes and checker-spots and hairstreaks, and the children from up and down the road would wander onto the Harrises' porch. Mrs. Harris would serve lemonade and cookies in the shapes of flowers and butterflies of no known species. Mr. Harris would sit in his chair and arrange his day's catch, and Mrs. Harris would teach my cousins and me to do needlework. We sat for hours, scowling with concentration, cross-stitching cute little scenes and heartfelt sayings on squares of linen. Mrs. Harris's knitting needles would go *click click click,* Mr. Harris would deftly pin butterfly after butterfly into the grooves on his cork spreading boards, and the ice would melt in our thin lemonade glasses.

Mrs. Harris finished our sweaters, but it turned out she had made them all in her shape and size — short and wide. My stringy arms and knobby wrists sticking out of the dainty little pink cable-stitched sleeves had a startling effect, like one of those clever tricks of mimicry butterflies use to frighten birds.

And after many weeks my sampler was finished. Through the snagged threads and blood stains you could barely make out the words HOME SWEET HOME. Below, what was supposed to be a cute pot-bellied wood cookstove in a cozy country kitchen looked like a wrecked 1941 Ford in a scrap yard. My clever cousins moved on to crewel embroidery and petit point, but for my second project, Mrs. Harris tactfully started me on something called huck toweling, which turned out to be nothing but a dishrag on which I was to stitch a border of giant red X's. After many rows I got tired of red and looked with longing at the shimmering pinks and dense purples of my cousins' satin-stitched Persian flowers. But Mrs. Harris said I must set a goal for myself. When my X's reached a certain standard of consistency, then I could switch to green thread, "for a nice Christmasy effect," she said. By the time I got to green, my cousins were doing appliqué and cutwork, and something called tatting, which resulted in long bands of delicate lace.

In spite of the humiliating needlework, I kept going back again and again to the Harrises' porch that summer. I kept going back because on some afternoons Mr. Harris would tell about his adventures as a young lepidopterist. He would tell about his mentor and friend, Professor P. W. Fattig, and their entomological expeditions together. He told about the time an enormous beetle, unknown and undescribed in the scientific literature, flew by right in front of him and Professor Fattig and then disappeared in the swampy thickets.

Mr. Harris's voice fell to a husky whisper: " 'Harris,' Professor Fattig said to me, 'did you see that?'

" 'Fattig,' I said to Professor Fattig, 'I did.' "

Mr. Harris was a wonderful storyteller, and as the afternoon wore on, my red and green X's would begin to loop and tumble over each over, until finally, when Mr. Harris got to the story of Professor Fattig and the wasp with the inch-long stinger, I wove my needle into the huck toweling, folded my hands, and just listened.

The next summer Mr. Harris rescued me from the torment of needlework by inviting me to come with him to catch butterflies. He was very particular about his recordkeeping; after every capture he noted down the time of day, location, date, and any unusual circumstances. He showed me the yucca plant, host to the *Megathymus harrisi*, a skipper butterfly that had been named for Mr. Harris after his observations of it in its pupal stage proved it to be a distinct species from the similar-appearing *Megathymus cofaqui*. In the backyard of the Harrises' little cabin we planted a butterfly garden — buddleia, pentas, and lantana for their nectar; and rabbit tobacco and passionflower, the food plants for the larvae of the gulf fritillary and painted lady. For the monarchs, Mr. Harris brought down from Atlanta a special tall-growing variety of milkweed I had never seen before.

By the end of that summer, Mr. Harris's work on the butterflies of the coastal region was complete, and the Harrises gave up their little cabin. The next year his book, *Butterflies of Georgia*, was published. Not long after that Mr. Harris's mind began to wander. He didn't know me when I went to Atlanta to see him. Then he didn't know Mrs. Harris. She got too frail to take care of him at home, and he was put in a nursing home. By the end of his life he had forgotten everything he had ever known about butterflies.

Every year when school starts in September, I teach a special science unit to my first graders called Butterflies of Georgia. I try to teach them everything I learned from Mr. Harris in those summers of listening to his stories and holding his notebook and his killing jar while he dashed through the woods making wild swats with his big net.

The little house up the road that the

Harrises rented for those summers is gone now, and wisteria has taken over the yard, but those milkweed plants Mr. Harris brought down from Atlanta reseed every year, and in August and September the woods and fields around the house site are transformed into a monarch butterfly paradise. The butterflies are everywhere, floating over the red and yellow flower clusters with their characteristic leisurely glide, looping and soaring and lighting and laying eggs. The plants are covered with monarch larvae of all sizes, fatly munching out neat half-moons from the edges of the leaves. The chrysalides hang like little jewels, changing color according to the light — lime green, emerald green, aqua green — with the golden spots and perfect golden stitching around the caps glinting and flashing.

I feel a kind of reverence in late summer when I visit that abandoned butterfly garden. I feel cheered and comforted, as if, somewhere up in heaven, with his tattered nets and stretching boards, an old lepidopterist is still looking after me.

Spelunking in Middle Age

There I went, crawling on my hands and knees, the light strapped to my forehead illuminating the rump of the spelunker in front of me. At times the tunnel walls were so tight we had to turn sideways and shove ourselves through by paddling against the ground with our feet. At other times the ceiling was so low we had to lie flat on our bellies and scoot along, our chins rooting up the damp sand. The stale air shifted from one underground room to another through this tunnel, creating a cool, fetid wind that smelled like damp rocks and bat guano.

I got into this cave by spiraling my way down a rocky natural chimney, my back braced against one side, my feet scrambling to find little niches on the opposite side, my hands grappling against the rough rocks. The chimney ended in the domed ceiling of the first room, and when there was nothing but open air below me, I just turned loose and dropped the five feet to the floor of the cave.

Now, on this hour's crawl through a tunnel to another room where I was told we would see "formations," I kept telling myself how to breathe: in and out, in and out. I kept smelling the bat guano and wondering two things: How am I going to get out of this cave? and Why did I come in? Could it be the same impulse that made me, last month, ride a mule to the bottom of the Grand Canyon, and yesterday send off an order form requesting more information on rafting down the Colorado? Could it be a middle-aged urge to overcome lifelong fears and dreads while we still have the strength? Could it be a desire to check out the many ways of dying so that when the time finally comes we can say, "Oh yes, I remember this one," and enjoy the meager comfort of familiarity?

We stopped. There was some muffled conversation up ahead of me. The tunnel had become so constricted that the first man could not get through. He began to dig out the sand with his hands. I squirmed into a sitting position, my shoulders hunched over, the back of my head pressed against the top of the tunnel. I pulled my handkerchief over my nose to filter the bat smell, and imagined the death I might have had in the Grand Canyon. The fatal slip, maybe just a moment of scrambling and heaving as my white mule tried to regain her foothold, and then the free fall through the clear air, the sky domed above us with the sun at its peak, the smell of sage and fresh air, and then instant death on the most beautiful rocks in the world. Here, underground, death would be gray and damp, without air or light, slow and strangling, with the little malevolent faces of the bats looking on and the smell of their excrement in my last gasp.

I heard the steady *scritch scritch* of digging, then some scraping sounds and grunts and groans. Finally the word was passed down: the space was too tight. We had to turn around. Scooching and slithering, we dragged ourselves back through the tunnel, back through the big room where the bats were hibernating, back down a hallway, to the room with the chimney. I stood underneath it and peered up. But there was a rocky outcropping over the cave entrance, so I couldn't see the sky.

One spelunker after another climbed up the chimney and out. Then it was my turn. Telling myself how to breathe — in and out — I hauled myself into the chimney. One foot found a step, and I shoved up, then one hand found a higher grip, and I dragged myself up a little farther. As slow and steady as a snake swallowing a rat, I rose up the chimney and out into the late afternoon of a drizzly fall day. I stood for a minute on the slope of the sinkhole and looked around at the dripping trees, their leaves just beginning to turn, and the dazzling green of the ferns and moss. I hardly knew the three spelunkers who brought me here, but looking at their muddy faces now as they gathered up their gear and pulled off their helmets, I felt like they were my oldest and dearest friends.

We walked through the woods to our cars, and I loved every step I took. I loved the tree limbs fallen across the road. I loved the red clay. I loved the little white farmhouse in the distance. I loved the chickens on their roost. I loved the row of collard greens straggling across the garden. I loved the teenaged boys who stopped their pickup truck and asked, "Did y'all go down in that cave?"

"Yes," I told them, "and we came out."

We stood around saying good-bye for a while before we got in our cars. One of the spelunkers began talking about another cave in another county. There a tight crawl through a tunnel, he said, but then a room with beautiful formations, the most amazing boulders, and transparent stalactites.

An old man came out of the little white farmhouse across the road, sat down in a chair on the porch, folded his hands over his belly, and looked out at the rain. He began to rock. I loved that old man.

"Can I come too?" I asked.

Computer School

One fall day all the teachers in my school system were called to a meeting at the Central Office. Paul Lewis, our curriculum director, stood at the front of the room looking serious and important in his mustache and tweed suit. He gave a stern speech about how it was time we "got with it." We all thought he was going to start in on us about how test scores had been dropping, or about consistency in lesson planning. But, no, he had called us together to announce that we were about to enter the computer age. By the end of the year, he said, he would expect all the teachers in the school system to have their class records on computer files. The school board had signed up a computer professor from Hadleyfield Community College to come down and give computer lessons every Tuesday and Thursday night from five to ten. Two teachers from each school would be chosen to attend the computer class. After the class was over, those teachers would conduct a computer workshop at their own schools to teach the other teachers what they had learned.

The next day I was not surprised to find a letter in my school mailbox telling me that I had been chosen to attend the computer class. I was not surprised to see an identical envelope in Mrs. Boatwright's mailbox above mine. I am always chosen for these after-school projects because I don't have a husband and children to feed, and Mrs. Boatwright is always chosen because everybody knows she's game for anything.

Mrs. Boatwright is big and fat. She makes all her own dresses out of cloth she buys by the bolt from Kmart. She prefers bright colors in floral patterns or wide stripes. She is not a skilled seamstress, and the dresses are made of two huge rectangles sewn together with faced openings for the neck and arms. Mrs. Boatwright is the only woman I know who still wears garters to hold up her stockings. "Mr. Boatwright doesn't believe in panty hose," she says.

Mrs. Boatwright is an old-fashioned teacher and does her job with a vigor and fierceness that is going out of style. Not a child leaves her third-grade class in June until he can say the multiplication tables through the twelves, recite the Preamble to the Constitution, and use nominative- and objective-case pronouns correctly in speaking and writing. Her students also have a lot of fun making electricity with Mrs. Boatwright's old Van de Graaff generator on crisp fall days, they hatch duck eggs in the spring, and on the last day of school they spend the day on Mr. and Mrs. Boatwright's farm. She gives a good solid education.

On the first day of computer school Mrs. Boatwright and I decided to sit together. We thought we'd make a good team. We were very excited. We had seen computers in use and knew about the wonders they could perform. Now here we were in a high-school classroom that was just bristling with them.

Soon the computer professor arrived. Mr. Wilson had a wide, fixed, and meaningless smile and a strange laugh — three *ha*'s, then a reflective *hmmm*, as if he were asking himself, "Was that really funny enough to laugh at?" It never was.

He started with the history of computers. He went on for nearly three hours. He told us the size of the first computer ever made and how primitive it was compared to the computers of today, "ha ha ha, hmmm";

how many vacuum tubes it had, what they did, the names of the scientists who operated it, the affectionate nickname they used for the computer in intimate moments, "ha ha ha, hmmm." Then he gave the same information for the second computer. Our interest began to flag. When he got to the third computer, Mrs. Boatwright and I exchanged an anxious little glance.

We had been at computer class for nearly three hours, and we had not yet touched a button on the computer. We had not seen the screen light up. We had not felt the keys under our fingers. We were ready to "boot it up" and feel the power of that ROM and RAM we'd heard so much about. Then Mr. Wilson said, "Now we'll take a short break, and then at eight we'll all meet back here for a little quiz on computer history to see if you remember everything I've told you. Take out a sheet of paper and number from one to ten."

During the break all the teachers went into the teachers' lounge to eat crackers and talk about how awful the computer class was, and to ask each other if they could stand it for five hours a night, two nights a week until Christmas, and worst of all, would they be able to pass the little quiz on computer history.

Mrs. Boatwright had brought two paper sacks with supper for her and me — fried chicken sandwiches, milk, two apples, two dill pickles, and coconut cake. It wasn't the kind of food you eat in the teachers' lounge, so we went out in the parking lot and sat on the curb with our knees up by our cheeks, squinting at the setting sun. Soon it was time to go back in.

The other teachers were there, ready for the quiz and the concluding two-hour session. We sat in front of Mr. Wilson, as attentive as warm stones. Finally the time was up, Mr. Wilson said good-night, and told us how much he was looking forward to the Thursday night class, "ha ha ha, hmmm." We dragged ourselves to our cars and drove home.

On Thursday afternoon Mrs. Boatwright and I were very glum. This time Mr. Wilson had a film for us to see that explained all about bits and bytes. We were drooping by the eight o'clock break. We took our paper sacks to the parking lot. The sun was going down. There were people milling around on the streets. I visualized the weeks of computer school ahead of me as an infinitely receding line of boxes, one box for each week, each box divided into two by a neat notch, one half for the Tuesday class, one half for the Thursday class. The boxes stretched in an arc toward the setting sun. Thanksgiving was the only break in the pattern. I squinted into the sun and chewed my chicken sandwich. Slowly the boxes began to click by. But as the most distant tiny box would come over the horizon, another box would appear behind it. There would be no end to computer school.

I looked at Mrs. Boatwright. She was sitting very still, gazing at the toes of her dyed-brown nurses' shoes. I wondered if she was seeing the endless boxes too.

"Do you think you can stand any more of this?" I asked.

Mrs. Boatwright said, "No."

"What can we do?" I asked.

Suddenly Mrs. Boatwright looked at me. Her eyes loomed behind her bifocals. Through the glass doors we saw the other teachers shifting themselves morosely out of the teachers' lounge and back toward the classroom.

"Miss White," Mrs. Boatwright said, "let's just walk away."

I felt a little surge. "Just leave? Just walk out on the computer school?"

"Now!" hissed Mrs. Boatwright.

And we did. We lurched toward the boxwood hedge and crouched behind it. One of the teachers came to the door looking for us. We peeked out at her. Soon she went back inside.

"What if Mr. Wilson reports us?" I whispered to Mrs. Boatwright.

"He can't report us. He doesn't even know our names. Besides, he's just paid to come from Hadleyfield to teach the class. He doesn't care who's there."

I was worried. I'd never done anything like this before. I was pretty sure Mrs. Boatwright hadn't either. "What if Mr. Lewis sees us? And what will we do when the computer school is over and we have to teach the other teachers how to operate the computer?"

Mrs. Boatwright peered out from the shrubbery. "Mr. Lewis is not going to see us. And we can learn how to run the computer by reading the manual that came with it. We can practice on the computer at school. Let's go!"

We crept out of the bushes. We kept on the shady side of the street and walked the few blocks to our school. We couldn't take our cars, because someone might see them in the parking lot.

We knew just what to do to get into the locked schoolhouse. A fourth-grade boy had been expelled for doing it the year before. We had to climb a loquat tree to the roof of the catwalk by the boys' bathroom, then drop through the transom.

We had no trouble getting up the tree, but the transom was too high for Mrs. Boatwright. By scrambling violently she could almost get her elbows hooked over the windowsill, but her shoes would lose their purchase at just the last minute and she would come plunging down. I got under her at the strategic moment, and placing one shoulder under her vast rump, heaved her up. There was some earnest grunting and scraping, but no upward progress. We sat down on the roof of the catwalk and let our legs dangle. Mrs. Boatwright was out of breath and had some bad scrapes on her knees. Her garters were down to her ankles. Her glasses were fogged up, but her eyes were sparkling.

"I know," she said at last. "I'll boost you up, then you go get a chair and put it out the window for me."

After that, it was easy. From the boys' bathroom we crept through the dark, quiet halls to the library and the computer. It felt strange to be in the schoolhouse at night. I imagined the grade-school-aged ghosts of former pupils peering around corners and giggling at Mrs. Boatwright and me.

Mrs. Boatwright was ecstatic. "Now wouldn't it be fine if real school were like

222

this? Oh, Miss White! What an education we could give in this peace and quiet!"

We found the computer manual and read halfway through it the first night. We learned how to hook up the printer and the disk drive. It was all perfectly clear. As a little exercise, Mrs. Boatwright computed her students' six-weeks grades, including some fancy manipulations for several weighted scores. We entered our class rosters and learned to call our students up by birth date, sex, and eye color. By ten we were feeling pretty competent. We climbed out the transom and walked through the cool fall night to our cars at the high school. We agreed to meet at the loquat tree the next Tuesday night at eight, said good-night, and drove home.

After the next Tuesday and Thursday, there wasn't anything we couldn't do on the computer. We would just have to remember it until the computer class at the high school was officially over, then make our presentation to the teachers at our school.

On the way back to our cars that Thursday, Mrs. Boatwright said, "You know, this is a pretty bad thing we've been doing, Miss White."

"You mean skipping Mr. Wilson's computer class?"

"No, I mean sneaking into the schoolhouse at night," said Mrs. Boatwright.

"But it's our own school," I said. "We haven't done anything wrong."

"Still," Mrs. Boatwright said, "it's breaking and entering. It's against the law."

I could tell she was pretty worried. We walked along through the dark streets for a while.

"I'm not sure I want Mr. Boatwright to know about this," said Mrs. Boatwright.

"Just don't tell him. You won't have to lie."

"But if I start going home on Tuesday and Thursday nights, he'll ask why I'm not at computer school. He knows the computer classes last until Christmas."

"Hmm," I said. "What will you do?"

"I thought I'd just find something to do on Tuesday and Thursday nights until Christmas. I'll stay away from home during the hours of the computer class."

"The library is open until ten on weeknights," I said. "Or you could come over to my house. We could work on the school scrapbook."

Mrs. Boatwright didn't say anything for a while. We kept walking. Finally she said, "I've been thinking about doing something a little different."

I felt something in me perk up. "What?" I said.

Mrs. Boatwright tried to sound casual. She kicked a pinecone down the sidewalk and watched to see where it landed. "Have you ever been to the dog races?" she asked.

That something in me turned a flip. "Of course, I've never been to the dog races, Mrs. Boatwright. Do women go there?"

"Yes, women can go now. They have laws about it. Women can do anything these days." Mrs. Boatwright patiently brought me up to date on women's liberation.

"I know that," I said. "I mean, *do* women go?"

"Well, we're women, and if we go, at least two women will be there."

"We? Mrs. Boatwright, I'm not sure I want to go to the dog races, even with you. I'm just not at all sure about it."

"Well," Mrs. Boatwright sniffed, "I absolutely can't go all by myself. And Mr. Boatwright will have a fit if I go home and tell him that I've been breaking and entering the schoolhouse late at night."

She paused. I didn't say anything. "He has a bad heart, you know," she added.

That was that. I agreed to meet Mrs. Boatwright the next Tuesday night. We would go to the dog races in my car.

The first night we just watched everything. There were other women there. They minced up and down the concrete sidewalks wearing high-heeled shoes and short, tight, slimy-looking nylon skirts. Walking behind them, we would be caught in the swirling wake of their perfume. It was so overwhelming that Mrs. Boatwright had to sit down on a concrete bench and fan herself and spit.

"Never trust a smell you can't walk away from, Miss White," she advised me sagely. "Perfumes like that are designed to mask the odors of filth and contagion."

What were these odors of filth and contagion? I wondered. I thought I might find out at the dog races.

We did learn a lot on our Tuesday and Thursday nights. We learned that it is not called "the dog races" by the regulars, but simply "the track." After the first night we found a bench near the back where we could see the goings-on without being conspicuous. There we would sit and watch the people stylishly lounging around, drinking, and getting into fights. There was a room by the office with cheerful red neon letters spelling out in neat Zaner Bloser script MEDICAL ASSISTANCE. People who got into knife fights were taken into that room. People involved in fistfights were dragged to the parking lot by men in red vests.

We'd been going to the track for two weeks before we started paying much attention to the dog races. Each race lasted less than a minute, and except for some shouting and cheering during the last few seconds, they weren't very exciting. Besides, Mrs. Boatwright thought the dogs were undernourished, and for several nights she couldn't bear to look at their pencil-thin legs and pinched waists.

"They're supposed to look like that," I told her. "They're greyhounds. All animals that can run fast have that shape."

"I don't care," said Mrs. Boatwright, averting her eyes as the dogs assembled with their handlers. "It's just not healthy to be that thin."

On our last night at the track we bought the Official Program for a dollar. It was a dimly mimeographed newsprint booklet that explained betting procedures and gave a little biographical sketch of each dog, including name, racing number, color, birth date, and past performance record. The program seemed like a mishmash of gibberish to me — vivid misspellings, run-on sentences, dangling participles, and columns and columns of numbers carrying to three decimal places. But Mrs. Boatwright, inured by years of reading third-grade compositions, seemed to speak the language, and she quickly explained it to me.

The betting procedures were the most complicated part. You could bet on a dog in any one race to win, place, or show. That was easy to understand. Then there was the Tonite Twosome, where you tried to pick the winners of the first and second races. More complicated was the Win or Place, where you picked the two dogs to finish first and second, in either order, in one race. But the one that really made Mrs. Boatwright's eyes flash was the Pic-6, a "big payoff" wager. In order to win, you had to choose the winners in six consecutive races. But to make it more tempting, and more expensive to place your bet (you had to pay $2 for each dog you picked), you could choose two dogs in each or any race, or you could choose *all* the dogs — but only for two races. DO NOT MARK MORE THAN TOO ALL BOXES, we were warned by the program. In order to collect any money at all, you had to have picked the winning dog in every one of the six races.

I wondered why Mrs. Boatwright was so interested. I knew she was a good Baptist, and she had already recoiled when I offered to buy her a beer during one of our earlier visits to the track. "Good Baptists don't drink, Miss White," she had informed me starchily.

"You're not thinking of placing a bet, are you, Mrs. Boatwright?" I asked. "I thought Baptists didn't gamble."

Mrs. Boatwright was rooting around in her pocketbook for a number-two pencil. "It's not gambling unless there is at least a remote chance that you might win. I'm going to bet on the Pic-6, and I'm only going to choose one dog for each race. With eight dogs in a race, there's only a one in eight chance that I'll win any race. With six races . . . there's not the remotest chance of my winning the jackpot. I'm only doing it because it's our last night at the track."

When the handlers brought their dogs out for the Pre-Race Parade, I helped Mrs. Boatwright choose a dog for each race. For the first race we chose number 1, Di-mond Girl. For the second we chose Cracker Jak, because he wagged his tail. For the third race we thought Step-a-Long Sam looked good. For the fourth we couldn't resist dog number 3, Foul Language.

"At least it's spelled correctly," said Mrs. Boatwright as she colored in the number 3 box on her Pic-6 betting card.

For race five we chose at random Black

Booty. But for the last race we disagreed.

"Look at that pink dog in the middle," Mrs. Boatwright said reverently. The dog's color was listed as "white" on the program, but Mrs. Boatwright was right; there was definitely a rosy glow about him. But I thought he didn't look very fast. He seemed a little hesitant about putting his feet on the ground. Also, the odds board showed him to be the least favored dog to win in his race.

"I think he's limping, Mrs. Boatwright. Look at that funny walk."

"No, no," said Mrs. Boatwright. "That just shows that he's eager to run."

"And what about that pink color? Don't you think he might have mange?"

"Of course he doesn't have mange, Miss White. He just has a lovely pink skin."

She placed her last bet on the pink dog, number 4, Snow Flake.

Mrs. Boatwright took her filled-out Pic-6 card to the window, paid her $12, and got a ticket to hold. Then we settled down to watch the races. Although each race lasted less than a minute, there was a long wait between races, time for people to place last-minute bets, buy things at the concession stands, and time for the anticipation to build. Considering that this was not gambling, since there was no chance of her winning, Mrs. Boatwright was pretty nervous. She was maintaining her usual professional composure, to be sure, but her glasses were fogged up, and her garters were down to her knees.

Di-mond Girl won the first race. We weren't very surprised. It was just the first of the six races in the Pic-6. Cracker Jak won the second race. Mrs. Boatwright was very disapproving of the coarse and vulgar behavior of the other spectators, who would shout out the numbers of their dogs as they rounded the last curve. "Go four-dog!" "Haul ass, number three!"

"Why they do that I don't know," said Mrs. Boatwright, smacking her lips. "It can't help the dogs run faster. I think it might even be distracting to them. We really should have a word with them, Miss White."

I didn't like the idea of having a word with them. Besides, I really didn't think anything could distract the dogs on their thirty-two-second spin around the track. "I think it's just a way for the people to let off steam," I told Mrs. Boatwright.

"Well, I just wish they would keep quiet about it," she said, glaring at our neighbors.

I thought Mrs. Boatwright was being a little hard on them. She had never been bothered by the brouhaha at the track before this night. Evidently the Pic-6 was making her irritable. I kept quiet.

She got more and more gloomy as her dogs came in. By nine-thirty five of the Pic-6 races had been run, and Mrs. Boatwright's dogs had come in first every time. She was sitting squarely on our concrete bench with her hands braced on her knees. Her hair had a wild, frazzled look, and she was glowering at the track. I thought maybe she was having a crisis of faith, since it seemed there was rather more than a remote chance that she might win the Pic-6. I'm not a Baptist, so I didn't know how she would handle it on Sunday.

A light rain began to fall as we waited for the last race, but Mrs. Boatwright didn't budge. I was too excited to care about the rain myself. The dogs lined up at the starting gate. Mrs. Boatwright's pink dog seemed to resist being shoved into the box. Mrs. Boatwright didn't make a sound, but my teeth were chattering. Finally the bell sounded, the gates on the boxes flew up, and the dogs were off.

Blue Moon, the dog favored to win, was way out front. As the dogs started on the final lap around the track the people began to shout. "Get it, number six!" "Go two-dog!" Mrs. Boatwright's dog began to catch up with the blue merle dog in the lead.

Suddenly Mrs. Boatwright stood up. She climbed up on the bench. She shouted, "Run, you pink son of a bitch!"

The pink dog was the first across the finish line. The announcement came over the loudspeaker. "And the winner is number four. Number four, Snow Flake, the winner of race six." Mrs. Boatwright had won the Pic-6.

I drove home. Mrs. Boatwright was counting her money. She carefully counted out $800 for me and kept $800 for herself. "I couldn't have done it without you, Miss White," she said over my protestations. She had very tactfully forgotten all the mean things I had said about Snow Flake.

We got into town just at ten o'clock. The teachers at the high school were coming out of their last computer class. We parked on a dark side street and watched them get into their cars and drive off. Their faces had a leaden set to them that looked as if it would never lighten.

I thought about my $800. I had always wanted to take a teachers' tour of Washington, D.C. I wanted to see the cherry trees in bloom and the Lincoln Memorial. "Why don't you come with me, Mrs. Boatwright?" I asked.

"Actually," she said, giving me an appraising glance, "I was thinking about doing something a little different. . . ."

I'd seen that look before. I took a deep breath, and suddenly I felt as light as a feather.

Horror Movies

My father left home in the early 1950s to
write movie scripts in Hollywood, California.
My mother, not wanting me to grow up
thinking of myself as a pitiful little fatherless
waif, would take me up to the Rose Theater
to see his B-grade horror movies when they
came to town.

The Rose had been an opulent palace of
a theater once, with red velvet curtains and
a wide curving staircase covered in thick
floral carpet, and on the creamy marble floor
in the lobby, a beautiful mosaic red rose.
But times had changed, and the marble floor
was now dingy and gummy with Coca-Cola
syrup, the threadbare carpet was blotched
with stains, and the walnut veneer was peeling
off the old rump-sprung art deco seats. In
the darkness, big overhead fans stirred up
the stale smells of rancid popcorn, Wildroot
Cream Oil, and mice.

235

Some of the movies my father made had gimmicks: paper skeletons that seemed to emerge from the screen and sweep over the heads of the audience, or a "Ghost Viewer" given to each patron at the ticket booth. If you wanted to see the ghosts and ghouls and goblins coming out of dark closets in sharp focus, you looked through the red cellophane panel in the Ghost Viewer. If you were squeamish, you didn't use the Ghost Viewer, and the scary things appeared as harmless blobs of haze. I would sit in the dark, hunched down in my seat with the red cellophane eyeglasses clenched to my face, looking for traces of my father.

And I found them. The helpless blond woman who clung to Vincent Price and shrieked rhythmically every time a disembodied head floated across the room had the same name as a silly aunt of mine. The little girl who was buried alive with only a few hours' worth of air seemed strangely familiar, and every time the clock emerged and focused itself on the screen to show the passage of precious time I thought of the round clock on the wall of our kitchen. The names of towns were the same as towns I knew, and sometimes people on the movie screen would open their mouths and say things I had heard said only by people in my own family.

But the best part was in a movie called *Macabre*, when two feet stalked across a dark graveyard in high-topped shoes. Even in the swirling movie fog of that gloomy graveyard my mother recognized those high-arched feet, toeing slightly out. We went to see *Macabre* four times, and every time, my mother would poke me and whisper, "Here come the feet!" We figured the movie makers were so cheap they didn't want to spend the money to hire extra feet, and there was the screenwriter lounging around on the set with nothing to do and a perfectly good pair of feet going to waste in tan suede shoes.

Years passed. In the 1960s my father graduated to writing scripts for TV cop shows. In the 1970s the Rose was torn down and a new movie theater opened up out at the shopping center on the edge of town. The owners wanted to get the decadent old Rose with its vaudeville taint out of our minds and get us looking toward the future instead of the past. So they decided to give the new theater a name in the present tense and called it the Rise. The Rise is all on one level, with steel gray carpet throughout and comfortable plastic chairs that rock.

In the 1980s an office plaza was built on the rubble-strewn lot where the Rose had been, and in November of 1990 my father died in California. I had almost forgotten about my mother and me making our pilgrimages to the Rose when I heard on a news program about a futuristic plan to enhance movie going. Theater seats will be engineered to move ever so slightly to give the viewers the illusion that they are flying through the air.

But I am not impressed. What is the illusion of flying, after all, compared to the pure delight of finding your own father's feet in the darkness of an old vaudeville theater through a pair of red cellophane eyeglasses?

Frozen Man

Who remembers that five-thousand-year-old frozen man they found several years ago in Austria? For a few days his picture was in every magazine; reports of his clothes and accessories and speculations about his life were on every news show. But we never hear about the frozen man anymore. Our lives have gone on, things have changed, and other news stories have seized our attention.

In my town the big news this year is that they are doubling the size of my school. Walls are being torn out, the auditorium is being transformed into four rooms, and they are putting up a huge twelve-classroom addition, with gymnasium and media center, in the middle of the playground. We are all looking forward to next year, when we will be relocated into brand-new rooms with gleaming floors and spotless walls, and a sink for every class. But this year, we've been warned, the sounds of construction and progress may make teaching difficult. To help us cope, our administrators have been kind enough to send us to an after-school workshop on "stress management."

There are ten procedures for managing stress. I wrote them all down neatly. But last Friday during our spelling test, a giant earthmover like a mechanical *Tyrannosaurus rex* began digging up the old fuel tank right outside our window in the very spot where we had planted our tulip bulbs the week before. Dirt clods and bulbs rained against the windowpane. Robert Hadley got so excited he wet his pants, and half the class dashed to the window, spelling papers flying, and the other half started making fun of Robert, because this wasn't the first time. In the background could barely be heard the plaintive little voice of the one student who was still on task: "But how do you *make* a K?"

None of the rules for managing stress seemed to apply. Was this the time to "fix yourself a hot, milky drink and put your feet up" or "imagine a sunset over a tropical isle"? I didn't even dare try the easiest one: "Close your eyes and take ten deep breaths."

One of the things they taught us in the

stress management workshop has been useful to me, though. The teacher said, "When you get in bed at night, stretch out and close your eyes. Then imagine that you're floating in a clear pool. Imagine the water lilies gliding by, and the gentle breezes." I do that every night. But instead of the clear pool and the water lilies and the gentle breezes, I think about the five-thousand-year-old frozen man. I think about the tattoo on his back, his neatly stitched coat, his stone knife and his ax, his leathern leggings, and the insulating straw stuffed into his boots. I think about the seeds of his last meal still stuck in his teeth. And sure enough, just as they said in the stress management workshop, I fall into the deepest, sweetest sleep. There's something so very peaceful about being dead and frozen for almost five thousand years.

Styles of Dying

I have an old aunt who is planning to die soon. There's nothing really wrong with her. It's just a decision she's made. Several years ago she cleaned out all her closets, quit buying new clothes, and canceled the paper. Her children don't approve of her attitude, and they give her a brand-new pair of Reebok running shoes every Christmas and birthday. When I go over to see her, she's sitting up in a straight chair in her spotless kitchen, her faded clothes in tatters, her hands folded in her lap, and her two feet in those bright white and lavender Reeboks planted firmly on the floor.

"I don't know where they think I'm going in these shoes," she tells me.

"They just want you to go in style, Aunt Babe," I tell her. And I have to admit, I hate to see my Aunt Babe, who has lived all her life rather flamboyantly, just fading away. It's made me notice different aspects of death and wonder, if it were up to me, what would I choose for my Aunt Babe?

I find quite distasteful the insouciant dying of camellias, which fall gracefully from the stem and lie dead on the ground under the bush in great blushing heaps, retaining all the bloom of life for days. Armadillos are just as bad. The dead ones you see on the highways look exactly as they did in life, except that instead of snuffling and grunting around in their nearsighted way, they now lie peacefully upside down on the pavement with their silly arms bent at the wrists over their soft little bellies.

On the other hand, I don't like the death of gardenias either. The blossoms cling to the bush until they have shrunk and withered into brown slimy wads that require what gardeners call deadheading. Spiders, which live with such stealth and cunning, die like crippled hands, and dead horses present a disposal problem that belies the dignity they had in life. Nothing can dig a hole that big, so the old horse is dragged by the neck to a low place back in the woods, and all summer the foul breeze blowing up the hill is the only reminder of a sweet and noble friend.

But the other day I was walking along a high pine ridge way behind our house. According to the topographical map, that ridge is the highest spot in two counties, and in fact, the day did seem brighter there, and the breeze seemed sweeter, and the great boles of the longleaf pine trees rose up into the sky with such strength and stillness. And then I saw a scattering of old bones. I don't know whether they were deer bones or pig bones or the bones of a big dog, but one thing was for sure: They were the bones of an animal that knew how to die with style.

One day I'm going to go over to my Aunt Babe's house and coax her out of that clean kitchen and take her up to that ridge. I'll just stand her there, on the highest spot in two counties, in that piney breeze, and the white bones lying there on the ground will be brighter than her Reeboks. I won't say anything, but if I know my Aunt Babe, she'll get some satisfaction from it.

The Starlite Motel

THIS BATHROOM IS BEING CLEANED, the sign said; USE THE BATHROOM ACROSS FROM GATE B-1. It was a long walk to B-1, and when I got back to my gate, B-15, it was 9:41.

"That plane left the ground one minute ago," the man said.

I couldn't complain. My ticket said, "Present yourself at the gate at least fifteen minutes prior to departure for domestic flights."

"A woman on standby was mighty glad to get your seat," the man said.

I sat there in the airport waiting for the next flight, drinking water out of a bottle and thinking about the woman on standby who got my seat. I hoped it was a window seat, that the man next to her was not so large that he spread over into her space. I hoped that there was no turbulence, and that the landing was not too terrifying. And, most of all, I hoped the woman on standby

245

ended up spending the night at the Starlite Motel.

The neon sign at the Starlite Motel blinks on and off, STARLITE and then MOTEL, all night long. Underneath, a little red sign says VACANCY. There is always a vacancy at the Starlite Motel. There is no HBO, no pay-per-view adult entertainment, but ice is free, and the windows have screens. Outside each room there is a little rectangular flower bed of pink periwinkle edged with smooth white stones.

The Starlite Motel is in one of those vast internal states, west of the Mississippi. There is a solid-feeling stillness there, so far removed from the vicissitudes of continental drift. Sleep will come easy for the woman on standby at the Starlite Motel. Night will come rolling gently across the land from the east, and as she dozes off she will feel the slight, vaguely comforting weight of the continent pressing in on her from all sides.

I was sitting on a bench outside the little library in DeFuniak Springs, Florida, one afternoon when a young man came up to me and asked, "Is your name Electra?"

There was only one answer to that question. "No."

He walked on down the road, past the

old white Victorian houses on the ridge around the lake in DeFuniak Springs, but I stayed there for a long time, thinking about Electra. If she wasn't sitting on the bench outside the library at DeFuniak Springs waiting for that young man, then where was she? I could only hope that she might be taking a swim in the pool at the Starlite Motel.

The pool at the Starlite Motel is not Olympic size. There is no lifeguard on duty, but Electra doesn't need a lifeguard as she floats and drifts and twirls in the bright water all afternoon. A little breeze ripples the surface. But it's not one of these young upstart breezes that gust up out of the Gulf of Mexico and dart around foolishly, showing off. This breeze is an old, wise, steadfast breeze. It's a breeze you can count on, and it blows every summer afternoon at the Starlite Motel.

The other day as I was unloading trash at the dump I found, neatly folded and stacked beside the Dumpster, a whole set of men's work clothes, somewhat frayed and worn, but beautifully laundered — and exactly my size. I stood there in the overflow trash, holding the blue shirt up to my chest, and the pants at my waist, peeking down to see the cuffs lightly brushing the tops of my feet, and wondering what in the world had happened to that neat and tidy little man.

He, of all people, I thought as I shook out the crisp folds in a white T-shirt, would appreciate the sturdy cotton sheets at the Starlite Motel, the cool, smooth linoleum floor without a speck of grit or dust, the clean smell of Murphy's Oil Soap, and the John Constable print above the bed showing haymakers toiling under a billowing sky. He would be pleased by the comforting combination of generosity and spareness at the Starlite Motel. Only one towel, one washrag, and one thin cake of soap are provided per guest, but the towel is thick, the washrag is dense, and the soap is Ivory. There are only three coat hangers, but they are not permanently affixed to the clothes rod, 75 cents is not added to the bill for every phone call, and the window air conditioner has a clean filter.

I wore that man's clothes very comfortably all day long, and that night I thought about him sleeping an untroubled sleep, and dreaming peaceful dreams of great distances and ancient summer breezes and vast John Constable skies, just the kind of dreams you dream at the Starlite Motel.